EDWARD
SAID AND EDUCATION

This volume offers a deep interpretation of Edward Said's literary thought towards the development of educational criticism. Insofar as Said's academic career was built around the contours of literary analysis, Leonardo demonstrates how Said's work propels scholarship on schooling in ways that enrich our ability to generate insights about the educational enterprise.

The book draws from four main themes of Said's work – knowledge construction as part of empire, representations and reconstruction of the intellectual, the exile condition, and contrapuntal analysis. These themes cohere in providing the elements of educational criticism and placing them in the wider context of a rapidly changing sociality and educational system. The author reviews key arguments in the field whilst contributing new analyses designed to elicit wide-ranging discussions. *Edward Said and Education* is a valuable teaching resource for undergraduate and postgraduate students of education studies, postcolonial studies, and ethnic studies.

Zeus Leonardo is Professor and Associate Dean of Education and Faculty of the Critical Theory Designated Emphasis at the University of California, Berkeley.

Routledge Key Ideas in Education Series

Series Editors: Bob Lingard and Fazal Rizvi
Founding Editors: Greg Dimitriadis and Bob Lingard

Freud and Education
Deborah P. Britzman
Marx and Education
Jean Anyon
Foucault, Power, and Education
Stephen J. Ball
L.S. Vygotsky and Education
Luis C. Moll
Freire and Education
Antonia Darder
Literacy and Education
James Gee
Du Bois and Education
Carl A. Grant
Dewey and Education
Walter Feinberg
Edward Said and Education
Zeus Leonardo

EDWARD
SAID AND EDUCATION

ZEUS LEONARDO

NEW YORK AND LONDON

First published 2020
by Routledge
52 Vanderbilt Avenue, New York, NY 10017

and by Routledge
2 Park Square, Milton Park, Abingdon, Oxon, OX14 4RN

Routledge is an imprint of the Taylor & Francis Group, an informa business

© 2020 Taylor & Francis

The right of Zeus Leonardo to be identified as the author of this work has been asserted by him in accordance with sections 77 and 78 of the Copyright, Designs and Patents Act 1988.

All rights reserved. No part of this book may be reprinted or reproduced or utilised in any form or by any electronic, mechanical, or other means, now known or hereafter invented, including photocopying and recording, or in any information storage or retrieval system, without permission in writing from the publishers.

Trademark notice: Product or corporate names may be trademarks or registered trademarks, and are used only for identification and explanation without intent to infringe.

Library of Congress Cataloging-in-Publication Data
A catalog record for this book has been requested

ISBN: 978-1-138-30288-4 (hbk)
ISBN: 978-1-138-30290-7 (pbk)
ISBN: 978-0-203-73164-2 (ebk)

Typeset in Minion
by Apex CoVantage, LLC

CONTENTS

ACKNOWLEDGMENTS — vi

ABBREVIATED TITLES FOR EDWARD SAID BOOKS — viii

1 **Dis-Orienting Western Knowledge: Coloniality, Curriculum, and Crisis** — 1

2 **Teachers as Anti-Intellectuals: Towards the Reconstruction of Expert(ise)** — 28

3 **Pedagogies of Exile: Learning In and Out of Place** — 55

4 **Educational Criticism and Contrapuntal Analysis** — 84

REFERENCES — 121

INDEX — 132

ACKNOWLEDGMENTS

I write to be interesting and it helps to be interested in what I write. This book was first conceived during lunch with my former Routledge editor, Catherine Bernard, at the San Antonio AERA in 2017. I executed it with my new editor, Matt Friberg. Edward Said is one of those important thinkers whose work requires interlocutors and intellectual kinships in order to appreciate its full measure of power. Thus, it would be presumptuous to say that a study of Said is possible without the help of people who have listened tirelessly to me interpret what I thought Said meant by empire, intellectual, exile, or contrapuntal analysis. The first victim of my recitations is my wife and intellectual partner, Maggie Hunter. In the end, she would roll her eyes if I mentioned the word philology one more time. My graduate students at Berkeley were patient and considerate, putting up with my intrusions into their studying by talking about my thoughts regarding Said. Michael Singh, Jocyl Sacramento, Patrick Johnson, Nicole Rangel, Ell Lin, Gema Cardona, Blanca Gamez-Djokic, Joy Esboldt, and Alice Taylor always provided fresh eyes and ears to my ideas. The Critical Theory Designated Emphasis, including my friendship with Judith Butler and Wendy Brown, provided a collegial platform for my latest ruminations. The constant stream of speakers and impromptu conversations about ideology critique, the ends of neoliberalism, and the future of the academy kept me sharp and critical. My hallway colleagues in the Critical Studies of Race, Class, and Gender in Education always make me feel like I am on to something even if it isn't always true. To my close colleagues near and far, I am thankful to your warm reception of my intellectual projects as I take risks and move into new terrains. I won't be able to name everyone who influences my thinking and with whom I feel mutual respect, but they include Michael Apple, Jim Banks, David Gillborn, Henry Giroux, Kal Gulson, Roland Sintos Coloma, Deborah Youdell, Ezekiel Dixon-Román, Sofia Villenas, Tyrone Howard, Michael Omi, Charles Mills, Eduardo Bonilla-Silva, and Jonathan Warren. Special thanks to Routledge's Key Ideas Book Series Editors, Fazal Rizvi and Bob Lingard, for commissioning this book. Finally, to my kids, Max and Zoë. May they experience the music of a contrapuntal life.

ABBREVIATED TITLES FOR EDWARD SAID BOOKS

Orientalism, Said, E. (1978). *Orientalism*. New York: Random House.
WTC, Said, E. (1983). *The world, the text, and the critic*. Cambridge, MA: Harvard University Press.
Beginnings, Said, E. (1985). *Beginnings: Intention and method*. London: Granta.
C&I, Said, E. (1994a). *Culture and imperialism*. New York: Vintage Books.
Representations, Said, E. (1994b). *Representations of the intellectual*. New York: Vintage Books.
Out of Place, Said, E. (1999). *Out of place: A memoir*. London: Granta Books.
Exile, Said, E. (2000). *Reflections on exile*. Cambridge, MA: Harvard University Press.
PPC, Said, E. (2001). *Power, politics, and culture: Interviews with Edward Said*. New York: Vintage Books.
HDC, Said, E. (2004). *Humanism and democratic criticism*. New York: Palgrave Macmillan.

1

DIS-ORIENTING WESTERN KNOWLEDGE

Coloniality, Curriculum, and Crisis

> The starting-point of critical elaboration is the consciousness of what one really is, and is "knowing thyself" as a product of the historical processes to date which has deposited in you an infinity of traces, without leaving an inventory.
>
> (Gramsci, *Selections from the Prison Notebooks*, 1971, p. 324)

I first encountered Edward Said's work in the mid-1990s. Admittedly, I was a late bloomer into Said studies as he was already an international figure, his 1978 breakout book, *Orientalism*, well on its way to canonization. I read Said's work in conjunction with other radical theories of education, from Bowles and Gintis (1976) and Bourdieu's (1990) study of social reproduction; Giroux (1983), Apple (2019[1979]), McLaren (1995), and Willis' turn to neo-Marxism and Cultural Studies; Lather (1991), hooks (1994), and Weiler's (1994) feminist interventions; and, of course, Freire's (1993) influential book *Pedagogy of the Oppressed*, and the Freirean tradition that followed it (Freire & Macedo, 1987). Critical Race Theory in education was only beginning to make waves with the essay that later launched a thousand books (Ladson-Billings & Tate, 1995). It was an exciting time of intellectual engagement, a sense that radical education was possible.

After I cut my teeth with Critical Pedagogy, I turned my attention to individual thinkers and did a deep dive into their social, philosophical analyses as they are germane to education. From Paul Ricoeur's (1981) crisp prose on hermeneutics; to Terry Eagleton's (1991) sardonic Marxism; to Althusser's (1971) structural Marxist treatment of capitalist interpellation; to Baudrillard's (1994) aleatory postmodernism; to David Roediger (1991), Bonilla-Silva (2003), and Charles Mills' (1997) unflinching critique of White supremacy; and then on to Fanon's (2008) heart-wrenching account of colonialism and negrophobogenesis, I tried to make sense of race and class stratification in education while satiating my appetite for interdisciplinary perspectives about social problems that required the most sophisticated theoretical tools to understand. Sometimes noting the agonistic relationship between race and class critique, I nevertheless insisted that they speak to each other, occasionally coming up with terms or phrases that spoke to their co-implication in social relations of domination, like "racio-economic analysis" (Leonardo, 2010) or "critical raceclass theory" (Leonardo, 2012).

It was not until 2006, when the American Educational Research Association Conference landed in San Francisco, that I started thinking about Edward Said more seriously. At that AERA, I was a presenter for a panel on "Paulo Freire and Race" where I introduced my unsystematic ideas about Said under the rubric of what I then called "pedagogies of exile" (Leonardo, 2006). I sat on that idea for over ten years but I could not shake Said from my ruminations since 2006, his analysis of colonialism and imperialism having a decisive effect on my thinking. Although he hailed from comparative literature, Said's relevance for education became my interpretive task, this book arguably representing that attempt. For instance, curriculum studies since the golden age of John Dewey, John F. Bobbitt, and George Counts has changed radically over the last 30 years, so much so that the continuity is difficult to recognize, more accurately characterized as a discontinuity. Although prominent curriculum scholars, like Apple, Giroux, and Pinar, continue the relevance of curriculum analysis, the influences of Foucauldian, feminist standpoint, and post- and decolonial theories of knowledge, to name just a few, have shifted the field of curriculum studies in profound ways that make the continuity from Dewey to deconstruction of the curriculum difficult to recognize. In this book, I argue that a deep interpretation of Said's literary studies of Orientalism, colonial-imperial history, and knowledge relations propels scholarship on schooling in ways that enrich our ability to generate insights about the educational enterprise, broadly speaking. In the space of this book, I concentrate on four of Said's themes: knowledge, the intellectual, exile, and contrapuntal analysis.

A brief biographical and intellectual sketch of Edward Wadie Said's life is appropriate at this juncture. Of Palestinian descent, Said was born on November 1, 1935 in Jerusalem to a Christian family, thus giving him a minority status within a dominant Muslim population, although he would later become agnostic. Palestinian identity, in its grandest sense, became central to Said's scholarly and activist work, but not in any tribalist sense. An activist for Palestinian liberation and independence, Said wrote tirelessly for decades about his group's displacement and struggles, central to which is the presence of occupied territories in the Gaza and West Bank. In his youth, he traveled and lived with family around the world, including Egypt and later the U.S. where he attended Princeton University as an undergraduate and Harvard University as a doctoral student in literature.

During early schooling, however, it was not obvious that the young Edward was headed for greatness, sometimes too fond of getting into trouble and receiving not so subtle hints from his teachers that he was not disciplined enough or was into breaking rules despite his intelligence. As part of boarding school experience that took him from one elite setting to another, student Edward read rarefied European literature that later would become the preoccupation of the scholar Said. Eventually, he took up an academic post at Columbia University, New York, in 1963 in English and Comparative Literature, as the Parr Professor in 1977 in the same department, and then later finished his career after four decades of prolific writing. At the age of 67, Said died on September 24, 2003 after a long fight with leukemia.

Said is often credited by many intellectuals as the veritable founder of postcolonial analysis in the humanities and broadly, or the study of colonialism as constitutive of literature and other cultural practices. That is and to put it simply, he and other postcolonial scholars trace the effects, contradictions, and ambiguities of colonialism through philological hermeneutics and appreciation for language becomes paramount. Said was best known for his work on the history of Orientalism, or how Europe constructed the Middle East through literary and other artistic representations. His book on the topic was not immediately appreciated and as his reflections contained in *Orientalism* inform us, Said had some initial difficulties finding a publisher for his breakout book. Now "canonized" despite his own misgivings about such practice, *Orientalism*'s centrality in postcolonial studies would make that subspecialty incomprehensible without it.

But Said's influence is felt farther and wider than that great book would suggest, his elegant prose appreciated in cultural and literary criticism in general. His was a dissident voice about world affairs as much as U.S. domestic policies, love for music and no love lost for Derridean deconstruction, and unflinching interrogation of racism (particularly against Arabs and Muslims) while he was no fan of race essentialism. Among his great influences and animators include Adorno and the Frankfurt School, Gramsci and subaltern studies, Foucault and post-structuralism, Fanon and Césaire, and his affection for Aeurbach's *Mimesis* and Vico's *The New Science* is palpable. He was fond of identity but impatient with identity politics, became an icon for a generation of scholars despite his mild iconoclasm, and his long-time friendship with Noam Chomsky surprisingly never produced a major collaboration between them. Said was among the most prominent of public intellectuals but spent most of his life in private schools and universities. Finally, he was both a lover of European letters and its harshest critic.

The four themes I explicate here lead to my overall proposal for developing a program of *educational criticism*. Although I am not the originator of that phrase (see Eisner, 1976), I hope to provoke the beginnings of what an educational program might look like through an appropriation and appreciation of Said's work. And although the reader will have to wait until Chapter 4 of this book before I earnestly discuss the topic of educational criticism, I contend that *knowledge, the intellectual, exile, and contrapuntality should be thought together as indivisible parts of a program in educational criticism.* Therefore, this entire book is an argument for criticism's proper place in education. But it is not criticism as understood in common parlance as only a negative move lacking any positive futurity. As I will explain, educational criticism is the assertion of our human powers with the ultimate goal of humanization, even when, through Said, I argue against humanism's excesses. It is then appropriate that we start with the epistemic problem because educators exist within what many would consider, the "business of knowledge." For this, we begin with Said's problematic: empire.

Imperialism is one part cannons, another part canons. In other words, as Edward Said (1978) reminds us in *Orientalism*, modern imperialism was not only a series of military and material campaigns through the use of cannons. It was equally a knowledge project as a way to domesticate a people, control their history, and distort their representation through canons of knowledge. In short, to know a people is to exercise authority over them, affecting their historical trajectory and social destiny. As much as the Orientalist claims to have discovered the Orient, they were able to *invent* it through a chain of representations.[1] Seen this way, the general understanding of Orientalism departs from the Marxist tradition of academic discourse that portrays imperialism as an economically motivated and structured domination. Far from rejecting a materialist interaction between the West and the rest, Said inaugurated a significant break that opens the way for a different methodology when it comes to interrogating colonialism and imperialism. For Said, the Orient, which originally represented the Middle East or Near East, becomes a controlled place of difference, which the architecture of knowledge created by the Occident, or Europe, subjugates through Eurocentric epistemology. Understanding knowledge as a social process is key in discussing curriculum constancy and change. Said's methodology is thus an entirely new way to engage questions of epistemology in the history of curriculum scholarship and the process of decolonization.

This chapter first briefly introduces the field of curriculum studies, an area of scholarship that has a long history in the educational literature. Then, it transitions to Said's oeuvre, an opening that provides a theory of colonial-imperial knowledge first laid out in *Orientalism* and then developed in subsequent publications over a long career. Central to this analysis is an accounting for the colonial-imperial function of western knowledge, such as defining and delimiting the other as part of a larger process of dominating them. Finally, dis-orienting western regimes of knowledge suggests intervening in ways that locate them, displacing their Orientalist gaze, while encouraging a sense not only of being critical but *self-critical* in order to avoid replicating the traps of and desires for western thought.

It should be clear up front that Said was deeply immersed and embedded in western traditions, often referring to himself as conservative in one respect when it concerned the classical curriculum canon, not unlike his animator, Antonio Gramsci. But contrary to E. D. Hirsch Jr.'s (1999) misappropriation of Gramsci as essentially in agreement with him, Said and Gramsci were equally attentive to *intent* in addition to *content* (see also Giroux, 1999). That is, they affirmed the social function of knowledge, which for them meant a certain opposition to power rather than its petrification. Said stood at arm's length when it came to the canon, at once deriving pleasure from the classics while deriding their authors' elisions because "many of the figures in today's canon were yesterday's insurgents ... once they mummify into tradition, they cease to be what they really are and become instruments of veneration and repression" (Said, 2004, *HDC*, pp. 28, 32). Known to elude his readers, Adorno was not fond of eliding power and mystification even if his difficult prose could prove mysterious to his readers. An interlocutor of Adorno's negative project, Said wrote contrapuntally about the beauty all around us surrounded by a regrettable ugliness. Of the Frankfurt scholar, Said has this to say: "Adorno has throughout his work on music insisted that modern music can never be reconciled with the society that produced it, but in its intensely and often despairingly crafted form and content, music can act as a silent witness to the inhumanity all around" (Said, 2004, *HDC*, p. 143). This conflicted, intellectual position avoids a totalizing critique or rejection of western thought. Far from it. As with the raw material of language, Said saw life in music and music in life, but always a constitutive part of modern conditions rather than an escape from them. This basic pattern in Said's thinking makes it difficult to paint him into a corner, the hallmark of self-reflection and self-criticality.

As D. W. Murray's (1993) uptake of Hume suggests, western thinkers have shown the ability to reflect on the limitations of European thought, including the metanarrative of the transcendent self. In its place, Hume offers a heterogeneous, contingent self that "not only projected a nominalist and fragmentary self-experience but postulated a psychological mechanism to account for the 'illusion' of self-continuity and wholeness of the experienced world" (Murray, 1993, p. 14). Or as it concerns humanism, Said states that "attacking the abuses of something is not the same thing as dismissing or entirely destroying that thing. So, in my opinion, it has been the abuse of humanism that discredits some of humanism's practitioners without discrediting humanism itself" (Said, 2004, *HDC*, p. 13). Going forward, this move may necessitate recruiting western thought in order to critique its excesses and decolonize it. As part of the project to decolonize education, specifically the curriculum, this chapter explicates Said's anti-colonial interventions.

A Brief History of Curriculum Studies and Reform

First, it is necessary to contextualize this explication within the field of U.S. curriculum studies. Of traditional keywords one could use to describe an article dealing with the topic of education, along with "teaching" or "instruction," certainly "curriculum" would be a logical descriptor for many. Although periodizing is always difficult, Fredric Jameson (1988) reminds us that it is a necessary, even stubborn, exercise. The curriculum field was arguably inaugurated by John F. Bobbitt's 1918 book *The Curriculum*, which was the first book-length treatment of the topic also bearing the term in its title. Certainly, the celebrated American philosopher, psychologist, and educator John Dewey produced tomes of material for what may be called the "golden age" of curriculum studies (see Dewey, 1938, 2001). Vibrant and contested, the field of curriculum studies – perhaps eclipsed only by educational psychology – enjoyed central status in the discipline and its public discourse.

Originating from the Latin word for "race course" (see Kliebard, 2004), curriculum became known for the process of deliberation over the selection of educational "stuff." This stuff was first and foremost defined by a set of materials students would be required to study, thereby setting the canon, from knowledge to college. Interestingly, Said notes that "canon" has two origins, the first from the Arabic word "qanun" or law, the second from music, "canon as contrapuntal form employing numerous voices" (Said, 2004, *HDC*, p. 25). More often than not, talks of canonization in education primarily show a fidelity to western ways of knowing, of certain non-negotiables treated as universal forms of knowledge. For non-westerners, this usually means suppressing one's own knowledge system, cultural standpoint, or denying oneself the status of being a knower. Speaking of his own educational experience, Said (2000) remembers, "Until I was about sixteen I knew a great deal more about the eighteenth-century enclosure system in England than I did about how the Islamic *waqfs* operated in my own part of the world" (*Exile*, p. 391; italics in original). Self-abnegation takes many forms and curriculum decisions and knowledge selection become constitutive of the subjecthood students eventually take up in the catalogue of subjectivities that becomes available to them. That established, setting the curricular course is at least secondarily a heated debate about questions of skills, dispositions, and purposes of educational knowledge that the adult population would be responsible for imposing on its young. Curriculum-setting is co-extensive with questions about the nature of the child, their relationship with the social, the good life, and the role of education in creating an ideal society.

From Dewey's (1916; see also Counts, 1932) reconstructive pragmatism to Bobbitt's (1918) system of efficiency, from Rousseau-inspired (1979) romantic notions of the inner child to William Torrey Harris's (1898) insistence on training the faculties (i.e., reason), curriculum was part of national conversation in the U.S. It was and is a contested terrain, the child's intellectual soul at the center of the nation's salvation. One senses that the knowledge project was part of nation-creation and maintenance. The lively debate captured by Herbert M. Kliebard in *The Struggle for the American Curriculum* was best described as a stream with waves and ebbs that represented movement in the field. At any given point in history (and in the stream), we find a dominant tendency, but paradigmatic control of the curriculum was always part of a larger political struggle waged by politicians and, important for this book, by intellectuals. In Gramsci's sense, the war over curriculum was never won once and for all but was an ongoing effort to establish hegemony over knowledge. In this cultural pulsation of power relations, intellectuals played a key role in harnessing popular imagination and sentiment. As central figures in moral leadership, curriculum scholars represented the voice of expertise and experience. Over time, this rarefied status has arguably changed, the curriculum scholar now eclipsed by the curriculum bureaucrat (Apple, 2019; Pinar, 1981). At least for a time, arguably up to the 1970s, curriculum scholars were influential in helping set public school as well as university curricula.

By the 1990s, what is now referred to as the "cultural wars" took hold of public discourse as to the status of "official knowledge" (Apple, 2000) in colleges and universities. Following several decades of multiculturalizing the K-12 curriculum since the ethnic studies transformations of the 1960s, diversifying course offerings and requirements in higher education becomes an intense battleground. On the integrationist left, James Banks (2006) and others (e.g., Nieto, 2003) argue for opening up the western and male-dominated curriculum as part of basic, national education. On the preservationist right, Allan Bloom (1987) and others (e.g., Schlesinger, 1998) mock the "cult of ethnicity" as watering down standards, trading excellence for self-esteem. This turn towards a politics of recognition also did not sit perfectly well with the politics of redistribution argued by Marxists. However, as Nancy Fraser (1997) argues, those who suffer low recognition usually are not favored by material arrangements and those who are materially deprived suffer low social honor. As such, a certain architecture of knowledge is built around the twin themes of production and prestige, a one-two punch that makes Said's intellectual work a powerful place from which to begin.

Edward Said and the Colonial-Imperial Project

My purpose for sketching a provisional history of curriculum scholarship is to point out the co-imbrication between material organization of and knowledge ossification in society. For studies of colonialism – or as Quijano (2000) prefers, coloniality – this double helix is key in any critical understanding of imperialism's DNA. As Said's masterful (I use this term provisionally) accounting of Orientalism's scope notes, Napoleon's occupation of Egypt was a turning point towards modern forms of imperialism whereby an aggressor's cannons were supplemented by their canons. Napoleon did not only subdue the Egyptians with guns but also brought another kind of army in the form of botanists, historians, and philologists. Imperialism did not only use powder but also power or, if Foucault (1980) might prefer, power/knowledge.

Said's debt to the Foucault (1977) of *Discipline and Punish* is clear when the former affirms the latter's archaeological method, whereby rules of discursive engagement produce subjects based on their inclusion, as opposed to exclusion, into statements that do not determine but define their participation. In other words, it is through their appearance (in statements, in documents, in narratives) that natives as such are transformed into *natives*. Said (1978, *Orientalism*, p. xix) writes that this "will to understand" the Orient turned into a certain "will to dominate" it. France's ability to "know" the Egyptians brings the Orient and its subjects into view or existence, as objects of consumption for the Occident. They are brought into vision by a civilizing force capable of *super*vision. Like Foucault's description of technologies of surveillance, the colonial panopticon sees the Orient without being seen, writes it without being read, surveys it without being marked. This happens through writing and other forms of capturing the natives for nativist purposes, that is, of asserting European superiority over the naturalized inferiority of the Orient. But Said disagrees with Foucault by asserting the author's imprint rather than its disappearance from discourse (see Foucault, 1991). This is consistent with Said's "worldly" analysis of literature and other linguistic practices as not reducible to text but instantiations of concrete relations with their context. They function as representations of the material world, not in the reductive sense that compromises orthodox Marxism's effectivity but in a Vician (1984) recursive sense of play between cultural traffic, knowledge production, and human participation.

Sometimes credited with Said, postcolonial analysis does not signal a break from anti-colonial analysis as much as it is a shift in explaining its processes. Said is concerned with the same colonialism that provided Fanon (2008) and Césaire's (2000) problematic but Said's is a colonial predicament turned into a literary phenomenon. Its brutality is not only its capacity to turn targets of colonialism into non-beings but equally their disfigurement through metaphor and other linguistic practices. The worldliness of language, for example, means that annunciation cannot be divorced from the earthliness that interpellates it. Disfiguration happens when knowers are perversely consumed as objects in the Orientalist knowledge industry and ignorance ironically asserts itself as the only legitimate form of knowledge (see Mills, 2007). Said shares Anibal Quijano's (2000) turn away from studies of official, administrative colonialism and towards the "coloniality of power." Following the grooves of Quijano, Nelson Maldonado-Torres (2007, p. 243) describes coloniality thusly:

> Coloniality is different from colonialism. Colonialism denotes a political and economic relation in which the sovereignty of a nation or a people rests on the power of another nation, which makes such nation an empire. Coloniality, instead, refers to long-standing patterns of power that emerged as a result of colonialism, but that define culture, labor, intersubjective relations, and knowledge production well beyond the strict limits of colonial administrations. Thus, coloniality survives colonialism. It is maintained alive in books, in the criteria for academic performance, in cultural patterns, in common sense, in the self-image of peoples, in aspirations of self, and so many other aspects of our modern experience. In a way, as modern subjects we breathe coloniality all the time and everyday.

Not to be underestimated, the fall of traditional colonialism marked a transition in the modern world system of race from colonialism to coloniality, from subordination to subjectivation, from the transparency of power to its opaqueness, and, finally, from what Said (1994a, *C&I*, p. 23) characterizes as the reliance on the "business of empire" and "empire of business." Just as Henry Giroux and Peter McLaren (1986) describe curriculum as simply the introduction to a particular way of life, so we can characterize, with William Appleman Williams, "empire as a way of life" (cited in Said, 1994a, *C&I*, p. 55).

DIS-ORIENTING WESTERN KNOWLEDGE   15

Immigrants, refugees, and other categories of people enter colonialism as a structure already lying in wait, whether or not a colonial power administers a colonial state (see Grosfoguel, 2007). In short, the world witnesses the coloniality of power turn into the power of coloniality to direct life outcomes even after the end of the official colonial era. Just as the end of U.S. enslavement ended one peculiar form of racism and not racism itself, thus inaugurating another form (i.e., Jim Crow segregation) to replace it (Bonilla-Silva, 2001), ending colonial occupation does not sound the death knell of coloniality. For example, in the K-12 and university system, coloniality of knowledge continues. Although I would argue that multiculturalism is now hegemonic insofar it has become common sense, curricular reform is a cultural struggle within the new landscape of imperial race relations. The question is not whether or not multiculturalism is preferable over Eurocentrism, but what kind of multiculturalism, how much, and for whom (Buras, 2008)? As the uptick in Alt-Right and Far Right assaults on what they perceive as leftist politics in schools and universities, particularly public ones, suggests, the U.S. is on the precipice of a second free speech movement, this time from conservatives clever, sometimes cunning, enough to leverage the lessons of several decades of progressive identity politics. This confirms Gramscian and Gramsci-inspired analyses' (see Laclau and Mouffe, 2001) basic assertion that hegemony is a process of power, accommodation, and resistance. The colonial power of western thought, while not hegemonic, does not dissipate but goes politically dormant until a crisis in legitimacy provides the conditions for it to reassert itself.

As the national speech tours of Milo Yiannopoulos and other darlings of the right sweep across the U.S., we witness coloniality shifting to new terrains or "war of position" in the struggle over civil society. But this condition does not "foreclose any possibility of a final reconciliation" (Laclau & Mouffe, 2001, p. xvii). Such is hegemony: no hegemony, no society. The struggle against the colonial-imperial project is the rearticulation of hegemony, the horizon of a new common sense. One could hardly be against hegemony, as much as it would be impossible to be against gravity. The deceptiveness of New or Alt-Right discourse is its appeal to fairness, such as the use of symmetry, or framing affirmative action and its sibling policies as a form of institutional racism against Whites rather than an imperfect remedy against White affirmative action since the Dred Scott decision. This new struggle over speech and freedom, which contributes to the development of Critical University Studies, tests the limits of both free speech absolutism that allows hateful speech that is not legally hate speech and the anarchist tendency to stop fascist development at the door at the risk of limiting free speech. As someone who took his pedagogical status seriously, Said pondered university life towards the end of his career and life,

> It is still fortunately the case, however, that the American university remains the one public space available to real alternative intellectual practices: no other institution like it on such a scale exists anywhere else in the world today, and I for one am immensely proud to have been a part of it for the longest and better part of my life. University humanists are in an exceptionally privileged position in which to do their work, but it is not simply as academic professionals or experts that their advantage lies. Rather, the academy – with its devotion to reflection, research, Socratic teaching, and some measure of skeptical detachment – allows one "freedom" from the exigencies of life.

(Said, 2004, *HDC*, p. 71)

Said understood well the special but precarious place of education within the colonial predicament. The university is where students may read Austen and Kipling uncritically and Marx and Manning Marable dismissively. But as part of what Althusser (1971) once called the ideological state apparatus (ISA), schools and universities are sites of interpellation and possible counter-interpellation (Backer, 2018). The seminar room, in Said's case, is a place for social experimentation where the intellectual resists *idées reçues* only after understanding their author's psychic, epistemological moorings.

Knowledge and the Epistemic Problem

To say that decolonization is a curricular problem is to suggest that curriculum reform is part of the decolonial project. Knowledge production has always been part of the colonial project for it was not only a material imposition of a foreign or external power but a concerted effort internally to supplant an existing way of life with another. This means that decolonizing the curriculum is no less than decolonizing the dominant theory of knowledge, if not knowledge itself. By theory, Said favors a secular version not reducible to its abstract, even religious, overtones but theory as part of human activity in Vico's (1984) *The New Science*, which is that humans can only understand (and therefore undo) what they themselves have made. It shares a family resemblance with Lukács' (1971) affirmation of theory's place in forging critical consciousness as part of creating the world we can get behind rather than only describing the one we reject in front of us (see Said, 1983, *WTC*, p. 234). But neither is theory the same as critical consciousness, the second providing spatiotemporal context for the first as well as accounting for the untidy nature of historical experience that resists standardization through theory. In this sense, knowledge is less a thing of human nature than a thing humans do.

As part of undoing what colonial knowledge has made of us to which we no longer consent, the gift of colonialism must be returned with interest within a decolonial project that dis-orients the curriculum. In recent decades, multicultural reform has put a dent in Eurocentrism's hold on the U.S. curriculum. That welt has been noticed as its sentinels were awakened in order to defend their territory. Once thought to be something about re-indigenization of land, decolonization moves on to new territory, this time the realm of knowledge and cognition. It is one thing to remove the colonizer from the first and quite another to purge them from the second. For the colonizer's stench remains long after the denouement of decolonization. Insofar as the colonizer was able to insert themselves into every nook and cranny of the colony, inner city, or township, including the colonial subject's self-concept, a decolonizing violence of the same magnitude, what Fanon (2005) calls a "*cleansing force*" (p. 51; italics in original), must take place.

Colonialism redefined the category of "human" as part of the radical departure within humanism to reduce it to essential traits like abstract reason. Since at least the Cartesian *cogito*, which pronounced the mind-body split in favor of a decontextualized, rational spirit, the coloniality of being meant that cognition was a cog in the juggernaut of European, capitalist, colonial expansion. Western epistemology has oriented humans, as part of defining their essence, towards knowledge as a conquering impulse. This "*ego conquiro*" and its accompanying "*imperial attitude*" became a constitutive part of knowledge, practically and conceptually (Maldonado-Torres, 2007, p. 245; italics in original). In practical terms, it means a fundamentally suspicious and misanthropic attitude towards the other as a threat to European being, who must be stamped out or violently assimilated in what has become a perpetual state of war. Conceptually, Europocentrism has a virtual monopoly on what it means to be human, for as Charles Mills (1997) reminds us, within the racial contract European humanism is just as it sounds: only Europeans are humans. To make matters worse, the "educational racial contract" (Leonardo, 2015) is flanked by the "colonial contract" (Leonardo & Vafai, 2016). Even accursed Whites in the form of White women and the White working class, for example, retain the mark and possibility of being human; they are beings, after all. The radical cut within the denominator of the human made by colonialism within an imperialist ontology makes curriculum reform a matter of life and death as colonial subjects fight off forms of social death in everyday life.

Multiculturalism's successes notwithstanding, decolonizing the curriculum does not stop at displacing the western canon. Replacing Marx (tepid on nationalism) with Malcolm X (strong on nationalism) as canonical figures on the left stops short of considering the limitations of alternative politics like nationalism. For Said, the answer to the problem of colonialism hinges less on sovereignty and independence and more on *liberation*. In fact, he wonders what cost to liberation colonial subjects incur as long as the fetish of sovereignty defers it. Despite its insurgent status, in the end nationalism becomes a poor copy of Eurocentrism if it replicates the problems it aims to solve. In his moments of self-criticism, Said (2000, *Exile*, p. 381) sums it up this way: "On its own, ethnic particularity does not provide for intellectual process – quite the contrary." As a *contrapuntalist*, or what in music describes two or more independent melodies side by side in one piece, Said considers liberation as nothing short of coexistence. This is most poignant in the case of the Israel-Palestine conflict for Said, but contrapuntality is an ethic he follows religiously (irony intended) in other realms of living.

Contrapuntal analysis is not a cavalier, relativist, or feel-good point about making room for everyone in the rainbow collaborative. I will have more to say about contrapuntality in Chapter 4. For now, one wonders how Said, had he lived longer, would have made sense of President Trump. Following the logic of contrapuntal coexistence, curriculum then becomes an instance in the musical ensemble of learning how we live with others as part of living with oneself. He writes:

> We should regard knowledge as something for which to risk identity . . . academic freedom as an invitation to give up on identity in the hope of understanding and perhaps even assuming more than one. We must always view the academy as a place to voyage in, owning none of it but at home everywhere in it.
>
> (Said, 2000, *Exile*, p. 403)

The traveler's knowledge, secure but contingent, becomes a way of knowing without the ideological excesses of either certainty or indeterminacy. Said sometimes showed little patience for infinite play, Derrida being on the receiving end of some of Said's criticisms (*WTC*, 1983), as much as Said derided the chauvinism in what Freire (1994) once called "smug Marxis[m]." As well, Said (*C&I*, 1994a) does not fraternize with ethnic triumphalism when he pronounces, "I have no patience with the position that 'we' should only or mainly be concerned with what is 'ours'" (p. xxv). Said encourages us to be at home in exile and to stand with the exile wherever we find a home.

We need not agree with Bachelard's (1964) "epistemological rupture," appropriated as the "epistemological break" by his former student, Althusser (1971), to arrive at Said's basic point that the geopolitics of knowledge requires not only an inversion of a previous system but a more complete overhaul or transformation of that system. Decolonizing the curriculum through nationalism, even a counter one at that, is only one necessary step towards liberation. As Said (*Exile*, 2000) notes, one of the first sites of change after decolonization was the schools, such as the Arabization of the curriculum and changing intellectual norms, including values to be taught. The inversion of Orientalism comes in two possible forms, the first and more benign being nationalism, the second and more nefarious being Occidentalism. Having successfully avoided the second does not guard against the limitations of the first.

As an epistemological limit, nationalism encourages schools and students to become different but Said ponders the importance of becoming something else altogether. Said (*Exile*, 2000) fears that nationalism in the university has represented not freedom but accommodation, not brilliance and daring but caution and fear, not advancement of knowledge but self-preservation. Not unlike the Fanon (2005) of *The Wretched of the Earth*, who was apprehensive that the native bourgeoisie after decolonization would become a conservative force, Said questions nationalism's ability to change what Althusser (1971) calls the "problematic," which is not the generation of *new knowledge* for its own sake, even its revolutionary form, but knowledge as a *new theory* of society. Sans the science fetish of Althusser, Said calls for a new function of knowledge.

Likewise, he critiques postmodernism's attempt to knock high culture off its pedestal in favor of celebrating popular culture. This move may be a nod to studying former NBA player Shaquille over Shakespeare but it replaces one form of essentialism with another as a knee-jerk reaction to western knowledge and its pretenses, in one fell swoop. Here Said sides with the official party line of the Frankfurt School with respect to the culture industry (Horkheimer & Adorno, 1976). To Said, over-celebratory analysis of popular culture is intellectual provincialism disguised as the opposite of elitism. But worldly in his approach, Said is able to keep his ear to the ground as well. Apposite to the fury over Saul Bellow's incendiary comment (paraphrased here as "Show me the African Proust . . . or Zulu Tolstoy!"), Said shows his contempt for the former Nobel Prize winner's impertinence even as Said is able to admit Proust or Tolstoy's greatness (and Bellow's, for that matter) (see Said, *C&I*, 1994a, pp. 25, 328).

Classically trained in European letters from grade school to grad school, Said assimilated the European canon if only later to be able to interrogate it. He did not accomplish this feat without also enjoying in no small way the pleasures of engaging the "great works." He is not a cheerleader of popular culture and took some pride in critical judgment about rarefied art, classical music, and high literature without their fetish. Said was far more familiar with Leavis and Whitehead than he was with Beavis and Butt-Head. In this sense, he is as conservative as they come, something of which he admits being guilty. He was able to launch one of the most searing and searching critiques of Orientalism and imperialism, particularly in literature, only by going through, and not around, the great works. In order to accomplish this, he had to wade through what Matthew Arnold (1867) was fond of calling "Culture," or the best that a society has produced.

Traveling Curriculum and the Decolonization Movement

The Decolonial Group travels to Barcelona, Spain every summer to hold its summer school and annual meeting. Not to be equated with postcolonial scholars who might concentrate on the colonial history between European centers and the Southeast Asian corridor, the Decolonial Group focuses its assault on the relationship between Latin America and the handful of European nations that have a virtual monopoly on philosophical thought, particularly its epistemological roots. From Dussel to Grosfoguel, this second articulation of colonial criticism shifts the debate to another territory in the geopolitics of knowledge on the nature of what Walter Mignolo (2002) calls the "colonial difference." That said, I am not making a radical cut between postcolonial and decolonial writers as ultimately separate movements, even if they maintain important distinctions from one another. The "post" in postcolonial is by and large compatible with the "de" in decolonial; both are *anti*-colonial and *anti*-imperialist. Both do not reject Marxism outright but neither do they find its uptake of race to be satisfactory. For Said, Marxism's main contestatory framework between workers and owners of capital cannot explain what he sees as the more-than-economic strife tearing up the global social fabric, not the least of which is the role of imperialism. Although their points of reference differ and the decolonial scholars are more at home in the social sciences and philosophy department than the literary-based postcolonialists, decolonial and postcolonial scholarship converges on a common target of critique: Eurocentrism.

Decolonizing the curriculum or colonization of cognition takes as its starting point the critique of colonial-imperial relations. But Said, like his close colleague Noam Chomsky, was always clear that power asymmetries, while formidable, were ultimately not indomitable. Said (*HDC*, 2004) insisted on worldliness not only as a way to arrive at a text's immanent structure as indefatigably historical but as a way of being in the world, of being with others. The comparatist Said was never radically separate from the teacherly Edward and the latter made appearances now and then in the philologist's prose. In other words, the university classroom is a social laboratory for testing the integrity of his otherwise lofty ideas, such as contrapuntality (2001), intellectuals as amateurs (1994b), and the hermeneutics of exile (2000), about which I will have more to say in the following chapters. Always working against the grain, Said nevertheless promoted what Freire (1993) would have called "generosity," which guards against the bad faith that creeps in after decades of trying to explain the underbelly of a hidden history, a certain misanthropy and necrophilia. Although it seems the two never actually met in person, Said and Freire were conceptual travelers with a shared destination.

As a professor of comparative literature for many decades at Columbia University, a Harvard doctoral student in the 1960s, and with a host of boarding school experiences before that, Said has a sort of bookish biography. He experienced colonial schools in several countries, traveled all over the globe and was as erudite as they come. These travels were both literal and existential for the younger Said, an unsettling time that impacted his intellectual work and made the more mature Said less inclined to settle for silver-bullet, single-axis explanations about the nature of historical experience (see also Leonardo, 2013). Travel is the exile's mode of nomadic living and Said could hardly avoid bringing this constitutive part of his social conditioning into his teaching and opinions about pedagogy.

> Our model for academic freedom should therefore be the migrant or traveler: for if, in the real world outside the academy, we must needs

be ourselves and only ourselves, inside the academy we should be able to discover and travel among other selves, other identities, other varieties of the human adventure.

(Said, *Exile*, 2000, p. 403)

This is not the kind of travel one finds on a cable channel endorsed by Rupert Murdoch. And it is not the sort of travel that mainstream multiculturalism is successful in propagating, perhaps captured by the guilty pleasure of watching *American Idol*.

Said's traveling theory, as outlined in a book chapter by that title (*WTC*, 1983), encourages the practice of knowledge as unsystematic (in the sense of abandoning originary thinking), unexpert (in the sense of reconstructing authority), and unexploratory (in the sense of positioning itself against discovery). The de/postcolonial traveler remains "skeptical and critical, succumbing neither to dogmatism nor to sulky gloom" (Said, *WTC*, 1983, p. 230). This is a form of learning that differs from the institutional apparatus we call 'schooling' that is more concerned with socialization's teleological function than the educational function that prepares students for the 'incalculable' and 'irreducible' other (see Biesta, 2010). It differs from uncritical forms of ethnic-based pedagogy because a traveling pedagogy interrogates any essentialist arrival at questions of identity, ethnic or otherwise.

The image of the traveler depends not on power but on motion, on a willingness to go into different worlds, use different idioms, and understand a variety of disguises, masks, and rhetorics. Travelers must suspend the claim of customary routine in order to live in new rhythms and rituals. Most of all, and most unlike the potentate who must guard only one place and defend its frontiers, the traveler crosses over, traverses territory, and abandons fixed positions, all the time.

(Said, *Exile*, 2000, p. 404)

Not unlike Giroux's (1992) "border pedagogy," Said's suggestion is not meant to be a form of trendy artifice. It is a traveler's perspective without the baggage of tourist mentality. It is a cultural politics of responsibility for the other who represents no ultimate instrumentality but for the desire to coexist in a relation of difference without derision. It is not a fetish of the new in the capitalist sense of commodity production amidst the old story of exploitation but a newness that reminds us of the dynamism and motion of real, historical life. In Said's words, "Peace is the state of distinctness without domination, with the distinct participating in each other" (*Exile*, 2000, p. 172). As a politics of difference, knowledge is forged in the interstices between self and other, where the other is not the foil for the self but its contrapuntal partner.

If the colonial-imperial lifeworld is maleducative because it fixes knowledge as something to be discovered and then imposed, then the decolonial imperative is to insist on its openness. Just as history is there for the taking, as Freire always insisted, knowledge is there for the making. If the colonial situation is a process of layered enclosures, then decolonization is the unveiling of its harms through complete disclosure and then looking for escape hatches. Colonized subjects occupy a central role in this truth and reconciliation process, but there is so much distortion to their development that educators must at least be Fanonian in their suspicions that forms of self-violence, or refusals about what the self has become under the colonial regime, are a necessary part of decolonization (see Leonardo & Porter, 2010; Leonardo & Singh, 2017). That is, colonial regulation of being, from the Manichean division of people to apartheid in everyday life, subverts the colonized's ability to establish clarity about their predicament. For so long, knowledge of the world served the master race's whims, compromising the subordinate races' true desires for liberation, often aspiring to be like the colonizer in search of an authentic image of the human (Freire, 1993). Dis-orienting the desire to become sub-oppressors is at least half the task.

For Said, the mistake has been oppositional thought's ability to stop at the door of liberation by settling for sovereignty or independence. Settling down is seductive, especially after so many years of movement where the colonial body is treated as something to be carted around or displaced from one location to another. This was sometimes articulated with the educational system involving Native Americans in the U.S., for whom boarding school was a form of enclosure, physically and intellectually (Dog & Erdoes, 1999). It may be a natural reaction to desire stillness in its many manifestations, from nationalism to nascent essentialism. Traveling curricula prefer to emphasize the dynamic history that provides the backdrop of knowledge and pedagogy. Intellectuals may be able to fix or freeze it, but this is a temporary condition in order to answer the exigencies of life, university or otherwise. Said's de/postcolonial perspective represents a pronounced ambivalence that opens up rather than closes off potentialities, dislodges the potentate that has structured academic life ever since the first westerner walked onto its shores. It is an education worth the name, a culture shared rather than a superior one that hovers, and a knowledge defined by what it can reveal rather than what it covers.

Note

1 Throughout the book, I use the gender inclusive pronouns, "their," "they," or "them" in the singular form.

2

TEACHERS AS ANTI-INTELLECTUALS
Towards the Reconstruction of Expert(ise)

> It's not so much the over-proficiency that's a problem. It's the lack of alertness that goes with knowing how to do something well. Once you know how to do something quite well or you're familiar with doing it, a lot of times you automatically are falling into routines. . . . It's the switching off of your alertness that goes with thinking you are proficient on something. So the trick is to think of ways of surprising yourself back into hearing freshly again. And that's something that really requires thinking and techniques of thinking. It's something you can do quite consciously.
>
> (Brian Eno, 1990 NPR interview with Terry Gross, replayed Apr 26, 2019)

I would like to begin this chapter with a provocative statement: teachers should cultivate being anti-intellectuals.

Antonio Gramsci (1971) once argued that everyone is potentially an intellectual by function in addition to being an intellectual by vocation. But one senses that for Gramsci, the intellectual was still an expert, the exception being that he promoted the intellectual from different sectors of social life rather than its narrow and traditional version. In addition, Gramsci reconstructed the intellectual's function as a social critic, complete with a philosophy of praxis. Although this chapter is not an argument against the intellectual per se, "teachers as anti-intellectuals" calls for a position against the will to expertise that has defined the intellectual heretofore, including teachers. Therefore, I depart conceptually – but not politically – from Henry Giroux's (1988) otherwise helpful and important call for education to refashion the teacher-intellectual against its technicist and functionalist version. For this chapter, I take my cue from Edward Said's representation of the intellectual as a novice or amateur rather than expert. By this, he does not mean that some people are amateurs, on whose side we should be, whereas others are experts. Instead, Said encourages, "We are amateurs together, subjected to contingency" (2000, *Exile*, p. 6). In *Representations of the Intellectual* (1994b), Said relies on other terms to describe the intellectual, such as outsider, exile, marginal, disturber, shipwrecked, ironic, skeptical, playful, beginner, or stubborn. For the purposes of simplicity and to keep in mind Said's reaction to what he thought was fundamentally wrong with Orientalism's deployment of expertise, I will stick to Said's basic redefinition of the intellectual as a novice: that is, an amateur. This is partly what I mean when I say teachers should be anti-intellectuals, or *against* the prevailing notion of the intellectual as an expert. It is anti-expert, not anti-intellection or anti-expertise.

Said's book title, *Representations of the Intellectual*, is meaningful on at least three levels. First, he surveys the discourse on the changing nature and function of intellectuals over time. The book's cover, adorned with pictures of intellectuals from Baldwin to Chomsky, Malcolm X to de Beauvoir, suggests as much. Second, it takes seriously intellectual work as forms of representation, confirming Said's claim that intellectual activity happens primarily through language. Third, the title signals a longstanding tension in the relationship between intellectuals and the people they claim to represent, arguably reaching its climax in Foucault's pronouncement of the "specific intellectual" who, unlike the general or universal intellectual, makes no pretense to represent others. Deserving to be quoted at length, Foucault (1980) writes,

> For a long period, the "left" intellectual spoke and was acknowledged the right of speaking in the capacity of master of truth and justice. He was heard, or purported to make himself heard, as the spokesman of the universal. To be an intellectual meant something like being the consciousness/conscience of us all. I think we have here an idea transposed from Marxism, from a faded Marxism indeed. Just as the proletariat, by the necessity of its historical situation, is the bearer of the universal (but its immediate, unreflected bearer, barely conscious of itself as such), so the intellectual, through his moral, theoretical choice, aspires to be the bearer of this universality in its conscious, elaborated form. The intellectual is thus taken as the clear, individual figure of a universality whose obscure, collective form is embodied in the proletariat.
>
> (p. 126)

For Foucault, the vanguard intellectual or avant-garde artist gives way to an acephalic movement with an anarchist tendency. Inasmuch as the working class is the mass incarnation of the intellectual, so the teacher represents its pedagogical version, the trade union materializing into the teachers' union through, for example, Vygotsky's writing (see Au, 2007). Foucault's fighting words indicate a clear break in left theories of the intellectual, with which Said is in conversation. Said's preferred position is neither simply about a public individual who exists as a figurehead or spokesperson nor a private one since our words and deeds, once entered, become social things up for grabs and interpretation (see also Leonardo, 2003a).

The Problem of Expert(ise) and Trouble on the Mountain

The reconfiguration of the intellectual does not vitiate against *having expertise*, which teachers surely possess by virtue of their training and the state's investment in their credentialization. The question rests on how they *function* (i.e., not as experts), help transform the nature of author/ity, and displace the normalized expectations of knowledge as a form of imposition (Dimitriadis, 2006). Instead, consistent with a critical version of the intellectual from the Frankfurt School to Freire, the

> role of the intellectual is to be oppositional – which doesn't mean that you're simply opposed to everything, but rather that you're involved in the study (and to some degree the enhancement) of resistance to all of these totalizing political movements and institutions and systems of thought.
>
> (Said, 2001, *PPC*, p. 65)

Said's mention of "study" is key, as the intellectual's expertise that is gained through focus and the refinement that comes with it. Always erudite, Said does not reject *being* intellectual, if by that we mean a deep, artistic, and sensitive understanding of social life; being *an* intellectual is a different thing altogether, which historically has been ripe with contradictions, especially when they become state actors and defenders of the status quo. To Said, the whole point of being an intellectual is "to be embarrassing, contrary, even unpleasant . . . a quite peculiar, even abrasive style of life" (1994b, *Representations*, pp. 12, 14), standing "between loneliness and alignment . . . state of constant alertness . . . an almost athletic rational energy" (1994b, *Representations*, pp. 22–23). It does not endorse what William Safire, the former Nixon speechwriter and *New York Times* op-ed columnist, once called "nattering nabobs of negativism" but affirms the intellectual's all but lost bohemian character (which does not prevent Said from wearing the occasional tweed jacket). Said was not interested in serving as a revered adviser to Arafat of PLO, let alone as a consultant for "peace" in the Middle East under the multiple U.S. presidents during his long career, neither a pacifier nor a consensus-builder.

Right away, we must enter into an important caveat. *Teacher subjectivity and professional legitimacy rest on the public's perception of them as experts.* This is the educational credo and teachers rely on at least the public persona that they are experts: e.g., in science, math, or literature. There is nothing necessarily problematic with this more or less commonsensical notion and teachers have earned the right to be regarded as experts and intellectuals. But as I hope to explicate in this chapter, if not for the length of the book, experts exist within relations of power transacted through knowledge production, which in turn produces subjects of knowledge and how a person is, in some cases whole groups of people are, made knowable. Thus, teaching becomes an impossible practice in the sense that it resists intellectual closure (cf. Biesta, 2001, 2010) and Said considers teaching an act that goes against received ideas.

In a similar vein, while Said found the cult of professionalization problematic, he did not reject professionalism or participating in a professional culture, the pedagogue being only one. Said (2001) says that it is

> very difficult to be a teacher, because in a certain sense you ought always to be undercutting yourself. You're teaching, performing, doing the kinds of things that students can learn from, but at the same time cutting them off and saying, "Don't' try to do this." You're telling to do it, and not to do it.
>
> (*PPC*, p. 90)

Being an intellectual, like being a teacher, is a double move of using expertise to enable people, in this case students, to develop radical skepticism about being an intellectual in the first place, which is "what education is all about – to instill a critical sense, a kind of nasty, demanding, questioning attitude to everything that's put before you" (2001, *PPC*, p. 225). In this spirit, Said has often elevated the university classroom – and to this, we might add the K-12 classroom – as a laboratory for cultivating a militant humanist intellectuality. This means that research is not only a matter of knowledge generation but power regeneration or, during revolutionary times, its degeneration. One recent example should suffice for now.

The recent protest atop Mauna Kea Mountain on the Big Island in Hawaii points to the problems of scientific research being at odds with the local community. When the astronomical and scientific community, which includes a long list of collaborators including my own University of California, goes forward with plans to build a telescope with the world's largest mirror on what is considered by indigenous Hawaiian elders as sacred ancestral land, we see the enactment of power in its strident search for knowledge. In 2018, building of the 30-meter telescope (TMT) was ratified by the Hawaiian state government currently led by Governor Ige, whose cost is reported around 1.4 billion dollars and will expand the existing footprint of existing telescopes on the peak to about 5 acres. Mauna Kea's location is strategic for observations, its low atmospheric and light pollution among the best and its towering height at 14,000 feet is reported to be taller than Mt. Everest if measured from Mauna Kea's beginning at the ocean base. Once a jewel for military position in the Pacific, Hawaii becomes a coveted site for science.

The protest on Mauna Kea during mid-July 2019, which has ebbed and flowed during the last ten years, to halt the telescope's construction has led to the arrest of tens if not hundreds of Hawaiian elders. The movement has garnered the attention and support of politicians like presidential candidate Bernie Sanders and actors like Dwayne "The Rock" Johnson. To many local Hawaiians, Mauna Kea is the home of their ancestors, both figuratively and literally, as there are human remains buried there. The tensions come on the heels of the recent first pictures of the black hole at the center of the galaxy, M87, nearly 54 million light-years from Earth. To make matters more complicated, the enigmatic black hole was named "Powehi" by Professor Kimura of the University of Hawaii, Hilo, which is an ancient indigenous chant meaning something close to "profound dark source of unending creation" (Picheta, 2019, www.cnn.com/2019/04/12/world/black-hole-name-powehi-scli-intl/index.html).

Since spring 2019, the scientific community was abuzz with excitement around the *closest* verification of the existence of black holes ("closest" since we can only infer its existence based on the behavior of hot, spinning material outside its event horizon, called "accretion disk"). Indeed, staring at the beautiful photo (almost exactly as the theory predicted it would look – which showcases the importance of good theory) I could not help feeling something spiritual about Powehi, producing goose bumps about our genetic connection to the cosmos, made possible by a network of telescopes, including one on Mauna Kea. Scheduled to be the most powerful telescope in the world, the TMT is predicted to enable scientists to peer 13 billion years into the past, closer than ever to the universe's origins, 12 times the power of the revered Hubble Telescope. This established, indigenous Hawaiians also have claims to an origin story based on Mauna Kea, revered throughout the Pacific as the mountain closest to the heavens while having your feet firmly on the ground (Prior, 2019, www.cnn.com/2019/07/15/us/thirty-mile-telescope-mauna-kea-protest-trnd/index.html). Stakes seem to center on claims to knowledge, or at least its priorities based on indigenous epistemology when compared with science's.

Scientific "discovery," which is arguably a colonial trope (Leonardo, 2016a), especially in this case, does not sit well when Hawaiian indigenous civilization and cultural self-determination are sacrificed to the imperatives of research, which implicates intellectuals and their expert roles. I should also mention that the whole debate casts aspersions on indigenous epistemology's quarrel with and perceived animosity towards science, despite their seafaring ways preceding Galileo's invention of premodern telescopes. This might be a red herring. Regrets abound concerning the observational time lost since the observatory's administrators first decided to close the site that includes the Keck telescope, potential Nobel

Prize worthy discoveries sacrificed, and valuable scientific knowledge that will not make it into school textbooks each day that passes (see Macavoy, 2019, https://abcnews.go.com/Technology/wireStory/amid-protest-hawaii-astronomers-lose-observation-time-64901093). There is no telling how many Oumuamuas, "the first object from interstellar space ever documented to have entered our solar system," have been missed as a result of the closing. Indeed, this is a setback for the scientific community and its intellectuals after great anticipation of new knowledge being produced from the TMT.

But we have to consider this setback within a history of setbacks for the Hawaiian people since at least (and this may qualify as an understatement to some people) the first encroachment of the mountain by science, of which the TMT is only the latest symbol and hardly the last. The protesters seem to suggest that knowledge progress should not be equated with human progress when the Hawaiians' humanity is not respected. That said, in what Said would have likely found interesting, a teach-in university has materialized on the peak amidst the protests (Van Dyke, 2019, www.nbcnews.com/news/us-news/hawaiian-protesters-started-school-mauna-kea-teach-local-culture-next-n1038911). With a captive audience, local professors from the University of Hawaii system set up public and free courses focused on indigenous epistemology, local culture, and history. Puuhonua o Puuhuluhulu University is attended by hundreds of native Hawaiians and their non-native allies, showcasing the movement's resilience and commitment to intellectual life and education as a form of enlightenment of people by the people.

The politics of naming or labeling also deserves pointing out. Consistent with Freire's (1993) insistence on the importance of language, my own interpretation is that astronomers hesitated to "name" the black hole until they could officially "see" it, which in this case is indirect since a black hole is not straightly detectable. That said, this is as close as we get. Powehi was previously referred to as the supermassive black hole at the center of galaxy M87, which is a name not too distinct from the black hole at the center of the Milky Way (i.e., the generic name is "black hole at the center of galaxy X"). It is as if the black hole did not officially exist (i.e., remained nameless) until we actually saw it, although to the best of their knowledge, astronomers knew it was there for other good reasons besides seeing it with their own eyes through the telescope. In this case, the telescope becomes an extension or instrument of the eye/I that sees. It reminds us of explorers naming North America and other places regarded as "little Europes," before which they did not exist and were regarded as open space. The geopolitical implication is that if no White person has "been there," cognition did not take place: "New England," "New Holland," "New France" – in a word, "New Europes" (also "New Mexico") (Mills, 1997, p. 45). This moment of recognition comes with a dose of misrecognition as we are now obliged to call a thing by a name as its official identity, since Powehi could just as well have been named "the red donut." The global scientific team that discovered Powehi includes a White woman doctoral student responsible for the majority of the algorithms that coordinated the several large telescopes around the world to create one supertelescope, whom internet trolls tried to discredit as undeserving of the attention she attracted. In the case of Powehi and with the aid of experts and expert eyes, deciding on a name, an otherwise innocent event, may be called colonialism at the level of the cosmos.

Posting Up on Colonialism

Known widely for his text *Orientalism*, where Said (1978) studies the cultural apparatus of colonialism to document how the Occident controls the Orient by disciplining the knowledge that allows us to apprehend the Orient's people and traditions, Said is the veritable founder of postcolonial literary criticism. Decades after Gramsci, Said intervened with his own reconstruction of the intellectual and the problem of expertise as inaugurated by his text *Orientalism*, developed in *Representations of the Intellectual* (1994b), and then refined throughout his long and prolific career. Said's representation of the intellectual is also relevant for young people or students who enter philosophical discourse as amateur intellectuals, in both the chronological and functional sense. Said's problematic begins with Orientalism, which frames the intellectual as the incarnation of expertise and was central to the imperial project of Orientalist discourse. This western orientation must now be dis-oriented, which leads Said (2000) to argue that as a class, intellectuals are "badly in need today of moral rehabilitation and social redefinition" (*Exile*, p. 120). As a result, it is necessary to put a wedge between the intellectual and expert knowledge in order to avoid the temptation to transform a certain will to knowledge into a will to dominate others. Rather than turning truth into policy and policy into a "regime of truth" (Foucault, 1980, p. 132), Said (2001) writes that against professionalization and specialization, "the intellectual role is essentially that of, let's say, heightening consciousness, becoming aware of tensions, complexities, and taking on oneself responsibility for one's community" (*PPC*, p. 385). Until he succumbed to leukemia in 2003, Said was not sanguine about the prospects of what he derisively refers to as "so-called policy intellectuals"

(2001, *PPC*, p. 413), pessimistic as he was about the steady march of professionalization and specialization.

In some respects, young people are a strategic place to test Said's theory of the amateur intellectual, as they enter the practice of philosophy and public life as neophytes. As amateurs, young people embody Said's preference for knowledge as a project forged by novices embarking on representation as a non-impositional practice through secular criticism, which for Said means the absence of divine originality in the production of knowledge. I prefer to take this point figuratively, by suggesting that teachers, as adults, *assume* the intellectual position of young people (just as we may take the position of the exile) who have not yet been inducted as intellectuals, who often express an openness towards knowledge as learners, and who regard information with humility and uncertainty as amateurs. I say this because despite Said's reconstruction of the intellectual, it is reasonable to assume that he still reduces it to adults and excludes young people. This lacuna notwithstanding, which necessitates a parallel argument about children or young people as intellectuals on another occasion, in this chapter I will follow Said's groove that intellectuals – in this case teachers – are adults, with the added suggestion that they may also take the position of the child.

Before we begin in earnest, I enter into caveats about how we might understand the "post" in postcolonialism, which may be related to the post in postmodernism, poststructuralism, and the favorite punching bag, post-race thought, as a way to shed light on what I mean by the "anti" in anti-intellectual. It would be accurate to say that, by and large, administrative, occupational, or "official" colonialism is now in the rearview mirror, or the "after" of colonial administration worldwide. Just as the Golden State Warrior post-game show signals a chronology of events and breakdown of important shifts in game momentum, postcolonialism allows us temporally to locate and mark our current conditions. But far from the irrelevance of colonialism, the "post" in postcolonialism signifies a new analytical place from where to understand the *continuing* effects and *different* forms of colonialism. In other words, post is equally interesting as a spatial, in addition to temporal, turn within social criticism. Said (1994a) notes, "After Lukacs and Proust, we have become so accustomed to thinking of the novel's plot and structure as constituted mainly by temporality that we have overlooked by function of space, geography, and location" (*C&I*, p. 84). Just as a postal carrier travels from place to place to deliver mail, post signifies meaning that moves into a new place of representation. It is germane to note that metaphor's etymology is traceable to the Greek word "phora," or the agent or bearer of moving something from one location to another, including the transfer of meaning, and "meta," Greek for *beyond*.

Postcolonial analysis is therefore a theoretical move that allows educators a different look at the problem of colonialism rather than arguing for its disappearance. For Nietzsche, truth consists of "metaphors which are worn out and without sensuous power" (cited by Said, 2000, *Exile*, p. 72). Metaphors come into existence, illuminate what was already there but "forgotten in the heat of battle" (Said, 2001, *PPC*, p. 202), become overused over time, and eventually flicker out and die only to be replaced by a better metaphor, like the apparent last days of "modern" thought. Likewise, postcolonialism transports our analysis beyond a strictly material, military, and money analysis of the colonial enterprise by turning our gaze towards its cultural cognate. Like the Australian outpost that marks the transition from urban to the bush, or light and electrical posts that help us navigate the drive home, post marks the spot that facilitates what Said (*WTC*, 1983) calls "traveling theory," whereby analysis takes us to different locales, climates, and destinations.

Said's innovation marks a new theoretical space from where we stand to survey the territory of colonial analysis, this time as a cultural relation (and not in the expert way inaugurated by Orientalism). To pursue the sports analogy, just as a forward on a basketball team frequently takes their position in offense by "posting up," postcolonial intellectuals place us on a particular coordinate on the grid of interpretation consisting of different discursive moves to settle the score with colonialism. Finally, just as we post comments on Facebook and other social media outlets, postcolonial commentary inserts itself into a conversation *in medias res* and alters our terms of engagement with the topic of colonialism. In this sense, post is an action or a verb to indicate movement from one intellectual place to another. In all, post is a presupposition as much as it is a prefix: that is, with culture, representation, and knowledge as constitutive of the colonial project.

Therefore, and sometimes credited with Said, postcolonial analysis does not signal a break from anti-colonial analysis as much as it is a shift or transfer in explaining its processes. Here, I would like to put to rest what I believe is an oft-heard confusion, namely that postcolonialism announces the end of colonialism as a structure. It would be difficult to come away from any of Said's texts, particularly *Orientalism* and *Culture and Imperialism*, and conclude that colonialism is a relic of a cruel past. It is more reasonable to infer that certain colonial *stages* or *forms* have been transcended, unevenly and varied for some groups or contexts. In this sense, the post- in Said's framework is simultaneously anti-colonial. Beginning with the premise that to know a group within an unequal power relation is to exercise power over that group, ignorance and knowledge, rather than being philosophical opposites, are pushed closer together. With race in the analytical picture, knowledge and power are fused within the heat and dynamics of colonialism when the colonizer's ignorance **is** knowledge. Philosopher of race, Charles Mills, is helpful here:

> *Imagine an ignorance that resists.*
> *Imagine an ignorance that fights back.*
> *Imagine an ignorance militant, aggressive, not to be intimidated, an ignorance that is active, dynamic, that refuses to go quietly-not at all confined to the illiterate and uneducated but propagated at the highest levels of the land, indeed presenting itself unblushingly as* knowledge.
>
> (2007, p. 13; italics in original)

Turning ignorance into knowledge is the modus operandi of Orientalist intellectuals and imperialist knowledge, demoting other ways of comprehending the world as subjugated forms of knowing, such as superstition or belief systems. As defined here, the reconstruction of the expert in Said's project can be found in either the post-intellectual (i.e., postcolonial) or the anti-intellectual (i.e., against imperialist knowledge). It is in this sense that I argue for reframing teachers as anti-intellectual.

That established, what are the challenges to forging an intellectual culture with children and teachers in an atmosphere many would call increasingly anti-intellectual since Trump's populist bid for presidency? This problem notwithstanding, I hesitate to give into the temptation of calling Trump anti-intellectual since this move is liable to reify ossified notions of what Broderick and I (2011) have called "smartness as property," captured within the ableist dichotomies of "smart/dumb," "bright/dim," and "intelligent/cognitively challenged." It would not be completely wrong to assert that Trump displays a certain anti-intellectualism, at least as a political ploy to galvanize his base, especially when juxtaposed with his intellectual precursor, Barack Obama. I prefer to say that Trump's persona summons more or less White, male, bourgeois, authoritarian entitlements to intellection rather than confirming a certain anti-intellectualism, simply said. My provocation that education recast teachers as anti-intellectual is more specific and serves as a move against the role of expertise that has defined all theories of the intellectual until Said. Therefore, against this backdrop, Said's amateur intellectual becomes the antipode, if not the antidote, to the traditional intellectual, including among the left.

Said's analysis of the intellectual as caught up in the project of colonialism is decisive. As a methodology, he provides a way to proceed analytically to trace the circuits of representation as they rearticulate the asymmetrical power relations between the colonizer and colonized. It shares a family resemblance with Charles Mills' (1997, 1998, 2003) relentless assault on the social contract that reveals a pernicious racial contract. In Mills' account, the intellectuals who parallel Said's Orientalist are garden-variety western philosophers for whom social contract theory reifies an idealist and speculative narrative about the development of "society." As a methodology, the philosophy of the racial contract, which is not a theory but a description of an existing reality and a strategy to understand if not also to undo it, posits the basic methodological question of "How do we proceed?" Because social contractarians begin with the assumption that only Whites exist as persons within the terms of the assumptive contract, literally and philosophically, they must distort, disfigure, and dissimulate the existence of actual, living people, mainly Blacks and other non-Whites. The racial contract follows on the heels of Pateman's (1988) preceding and powerful critique of the "sexual contract," which prompted a more complete racialized-gendered interrogation of domination aided by the intellectual project of social contract-inspired research (Pateman & Mills, 2007).

Said's critique of Orientalism departs from Mills and Pateman through Said's focus on literature and art, and the construction of experts through them. This allows Said, in his own assessment, to grasp the daily, almost mundane aspects of power through cultural practices of intellectuals within colonial relations. By studying poetry, popular and classical art, low-brow travel writings, and high-brow novels, Said is able to trace the outlines of an imagined Orient according to the minds of western intellectuals, which are then flanked by institutions that confirm their representations as real and representative. He writes forcefully,

> For every Orientalist [intellectual], quite literally, there is a support system of staggering power, considering the ephemerality of the myths that Orientalism propagates. This system now culminates in the very institutions of the state. To write about the Arab Oriental world, therefore, is to write with the authority of a nation, and not with the affirmation of a strident ideology but with the unquestioning certainty of absolute truth backed by absolute force.
>
> (1978, *Orientalism*, p. 307)

Different from "intel" of governmental actors like CoIntelPro of the 1960s, Orientalist intelligence is subtle. It works at the level of common sense and representations that naturalize the intellectual's colonial ammunitions without ever firing a shot. Gramsci's (1971) presence between Said's lines does not need much teasing out, the Italian's profound critique of hegemony in advanced western nations forming an important arc in the Columbia Professor's opus. The creation of myths is not simply about lies and deceptions but the mythologization of truths that bind society.

But the U.S.'s distant and abstract relationship with the Oriental Middle East differs from Europe's involvement in colonial relations, particularly England and France. Said notes that in the U.S.,

> there was no deeply invested tradition of Orientalism, and consequently in the United States knowledge of the Orient never passed through the refining and reticulating and reconstructing process, whose beginning was in philological study, that it went through in Europe.
>
> (Said, 1978, *Orientalism*, p. 290)

As a result, by the time the Orient is intellectually captured in U.S. scholarship and governmental documents, it is less through the humanities and more through social science, therefore surrendering the powerful apparatus of cultural representation in exchange for understanding "'attitudes,' 'trends,' 'statistics'" (1978, *Orientalism*, p. 291). By contrast, in the case of Arab-produced writing, "[a] literary text speaks more or less directly of a living reality. Its force is not that it is Arab, or French, or English; its force is in the power and vitality of words" that speak to their ideas of the Orient (1978, *Orientalism*, p. 291). To be sure, Said reckons that Near East languages are topics of study in "Orientalism Now," but they are not dominated by the philological, but social scientific, species of intellectual work and therefore provide a "cachet of authority, almost a mystique, to the 'expert' who appears able to deal with hopelessly obscure material with firsthand skill" (1978, *Orientalism*, p. 291). With traditional Orientalism, we understand how Orientals are imagined and created subjects of culture, which is lost in the positivism of social science.

Once again, the problem of intellectual expertise is invoked. American or post-classical Orientalism is neither necessarily cause for applause nor more deplorable than the British, primarily, and French, secondarily. But in fact, the turn to social science hides more effectively the problem of expertise when positivism is recruited to scientize the Orient in order, for example, to reeducate the Middle East through curriculum reform, both inside and outside the U.S., making "Desert Storm" more than just a military campaign. Although Said does not spend much time citing or engaging the social science research arm of Orientalism, his point is interesting for it brings up important differences in forms of colonialism, their relationship with knowledge, and changes over time. As a case in point, Said has always insisted that U.S. involvement in the Middle East has always been more politicized than Europe's because of the presence of Israel and its alliance with the U.S. Therefore, American hands are less involved with culture in the classical sense; I say classical because Hollywood movies, sit-com shows, and television journalism do their own work in representing the Orient. As well, while the surge of social science writings about the Middle East is important, the popular or entertainment intellectual's role becomes ambiguous since the place of the culture industry, as Horkheimer and Adorno (1991) once called it, in intellectual life is yet to be clear, which does not suggest it is not effective. Bernard Lewis is unequivocally an Orientalist but Stephen Spielberg . . . not so sure.

With Said's innovative methodology, encyclopedic content analysis, and distinctive commitment to intellectual life as bound up with political life, educators are in a new place to understand the intricate transaction between knowledge and processes of othering. This new vocation elevates the politics of representation not as anathema to truth because arguing that no Oriental "essence" exists is not the same thing as the inability to recognize that power is deployed for particular interests. Said clarifies,

> My whole point about this system is not that it is a misrepresentation of some Oriental essence – in which I do not for a moment believe – but that it operates as representations usually do, for a purpose, according to a tendency, in a specific historical, intellectual, and even economic setting. In other words, representations have purposes, they are effective much of the time, they accomplish one or many tasks. Representations are formations, or as Roland Barthes has said of all operations of language, they are deformations.
>
> (1978, *Orientalism*, p. 273)

The *representative intellectual*, that is, one who is endowed with the specific and social function of representing with a public audience in mind, bears the ethical burden of speaking certain truths to power in a way that fifth grade Johnny or Stephanie does not yet exercise such an option (nor probably the expertise). For now, their turn will have to wait.

Representing the Post- or Anti-Intellectual

In criticism – whether literary, philosophical or otherwise – there has been an historical attention to the role and function of the intellectual. Among the left, in particular, a cursory look includes the following inventory and their proponents:

- vanguard intellectual (Lenin)
- the talented tenth (Du Bois)
- organic intellectual (Gramsci)
- specific intellectual (Foucault)
- native intellectual (Fanon)
- dialogical intellectual (Bakhtin)
- teachers as transformative intellectuals (Giroux)
- border intellectual (Anzaldua; Giroux and McLaren)
- Black feminist intellectual (Collins)
- Black British intellectuals (Warmington)
- orgiastic intellectual (Bataille; Baudrillard)

I do not have the space to delineate what each theory of the intellectual entails, but I wanted to paint a consistent picture wherein the intellectual occupies a central place in left thinking. For his part, Said (*Representations*, 1994b) offers his reconstruction of the intellectual as amateur to counter the focus on competence and authority that has marked the intellectual from Lenin and on. This has pedagogical implications, as I have been arguing.

Once a favored child of the elites, intellectuals have enjoyed rarefied status, particularly in the West. However, Said ventures that among the left, the intellectual has

> fallen into disrepute and disuse. And what instead has appeared are words like professional and scholar and academic. And the use of the word intellectual as a concept suggests something rather more general than concrete. If you want to keep Foucault's use of the word – he distinguishes between a general and a specific

intellectual – than [sic] it might come back into currency. But it hasn't.

(2001, *PPC*, p. 332)

Said's concern may be distilled as a weariness with the fetish of expertise that defines the intellectual as a guardian of tradition, and criticism as the practice of "great thinkers" whose ideas warrant canonization. By contrast, he prefers the intellectual as "a kind of Archimedean position of the critic, who's always outside of the group, who doesn't represent anything, but is a force for skepticism" (2001, *PPC*, p. 333). The traditional intellectual and their ideas are catalogued under the aegis of what Matthew Arnold (1867) once called "Culture" (here it is appropriate to capitalize "culture") or the best that a society has produced, which is opposite to its complementarity, "anarchy." Said insists that the intellectual as amateur works against the grain of literary tradition as part of a longer history of imperialism. It does not deny the amateur intellectual claims to having some kind of expertise, but vacates the will to dominate others through superior vision (supervision?) and originator of meaning that has become the cult of expertise in academic work. In fact, it is telling and therefore lacking in irony that Said's critic, Bernard Lewis, discredits the literary comparatist Said as insufficiently expert in Area Studies. The reconstruction of the expert reminds us that Vygotsky's (1978) experimental research on "*legitimate peripheral participation*" (Lave & Wenger, 1991, p. 29; italics in original) was decisive in reworking the nature of classroom expertise. Despite this, Vygostky's cultural psychological program is still tethered to the idea of young students eventually becoming experts with the assistance of more capable learners like teachers, moving them from periphery to center. Said's oppositional intellectual is permanently peripheral, ex-centric (i.e., outside the center), and chooses marginality.

Against the religiosity of "sacred texts" (i.e., the canon), Said's move towards secular criticism attempts to dismantle the dominatory tradition of intellectual work that is the hallmark of Orientalist discourse and other modern imperialist projects, including its favored association with the intellectual. Influenced by the Foucault (1977) of *Discipline and Punish*, Said's *Orientalism* appears on the intellectual scene only a year later. Early on in what became a long and distinguished career, Said casts aspersions on the disciplinary functions of knowledge in reproducing power relations between the Occident and Orient whereby the second is caricatured, reduced, and infantilized through the expertise of the first for its own pleasures and political interests. The upshot is that in addition to military prowess, Europeans are able to dominate the Near East through an educative, cultural process. Unable to separate themselves from the imperial project, intellectuals joined the military when Napoleon brought scholars and artists with him when he conquered Egypt. But more generally, Said's opening excavates the imperial project through intellectual work and his readings of haute literature, whether it be Jane Austen or Joseph Conrad, are symptomatic of the symbiotic relationship between the gun and the pen. In other words, his work suggests that imperialism is one-part military, one-part literary.

Relying on expertise, the Orientalist's authority is built on the power to be *there* in the Orient in order to catalogue, survey, and define it, and by doing so, construct the Orient as a weak mimesis of Europe. This is an important distinguishing feature in the difference between English and American Orientalism, or "presence" in the Middle East. Whereas England played a direct role in places like India through colonialism, the U.S.'s role is more abstract, more distant, and concentrated on policies involving the presence of Israel. Even French Orientalism was indirect until the last decades of the nineteenth century. So being *there* is an important part of traditional Orientalist methodology because a claim to objectivity and experience in the Orient can be leveraged, whereas world powers like the U.S. do not pretend to be "insiders" in the Middle East. In the Orientalist perspective, "The Orient is not at all a place where modern Orientals live, work, produce; it is a cocoon cloistered away from the real modern world" (Said, 2001, *PPC*, p. 27). This is further evidence that postcolonial theory privileges geo-spatial, rather than temporal, analysis.

In the U.S., the cultural wars during the 1990s is evidence of what I might call a certain "urban Orientalism" wherein knowledge about Black and Latino communities were largely defined and derided by White academics and policymakers. These patterned portraits provoked Robin D. G. Kelley's (see Kelley, 1998) incendiary book title, *Yo Mama's Disfunktional!* As research on urban communities since at least the 1960s was dominated by White academics, a distorted portrait of Black and Latinx Americans was almost predictable. Just as the Orient became a place described by the expert Orientalist as immature and immaterial, urban America was "captured" as criminal and crack-ridden through self-referential documents from the Moynihan Report onwards to the underclass debates of the 1980s–1990s. And just as the Orientalist industry was a European or White dominant field, so too was the writing on the "urban problem," including in education (see Brown, 2011; Leonardo & Hunter, 2007). Consequently, although many accounts did not expressly try to influence policy (the Moynihan Report did), social scientific research, including ethnographies of urban communities, started to drive policy conversations, resulting in the war against poverty, later the war against drugs, and finally the war against schools (Leonardo, 2007). Just as we cannot draw a direct line from Austen to Algeria, or from Oscar Lewis to Oakland, the methodology of urban Orientalism that speaks of culture absent references to imperialist structures, facilitates the dominatory function of knowledge. The pen may not have pulled the trigger but the arsenal of criminalized images of urban communities and people of color loaded the gun with bullets. Intellectual life conspires with social life.

For Said, intellectual practice is not characterized by apprehending a truth that never arrives. Rather, he asks what kind of work representations do and accomplish in the world, because "it does not finally matter *who* wrote what, but rather *how* a work is written and *how* it is read" (Said, 2000, *Exile*, p. 385; italics in original). It is not simply a case of misunderstanding the Orient because Orientalists never really endeavored to understand it correctly in the first place. Said does not argue that great European letters caused imperialism in any corresponding way. That would be trite and reductive, and he admires European letters despite their collusion with colonialism. He distinguishes,

> No, cultural forms like the novel or the opera do not cause people to go out and imperialize – Carlyle did not drive Rhodes directly and he certainly cannot be "blamed" for the problems in today's southern Africa – but it is genuinely troubling to see how little Britain's great humanistic ideas, institutions, and monuments, which we still celebrate as having the power ahistorically to command our approval, how little they stand in the way of the accelerating imperial process.
>
> (1994a, *C&I*, pp. 81–82)

In other words, any intellectual knows the power of leveraging ideological representations, however, they do not, by themselves, cause either colonialism or spur on people to colonize other people. But neither does the work of intellectuals freely float in interpretive space, especially when they are buoyed by claims to expertise, glossed by presumptions of objectivity, invested with power, and articulated with institutions. Said (1994a) expands, "I am not trying to say that the novel – or the culture in the broad sense – 'caused' imperialism, but that the novel, as a cultural artefact of bourgeois society, and imperialism are unthinkable without each other" (*C&I*, pp. 70–71). The West's tendencies and attitude facilitate its ability to enact, consolidate, and then enjoy its imperial powers. In this process, work of traditional intellectuals, from novelists to artists, imposes an order to an experience that by and large exists without a determining structure and by doing so, enables the Orient to come into view, albeit distorted.

The post or anti-intellectual's project, as laid out in Said's pedagogy and appropriated here, suggests coming to terms with the multiple attempts by intellectuals themselves to elevate not only the adroit but expert observations of thought leaders. Educators may find much purchase in this new representation but it departs from even the most insurgent and progressive rehabilitations of the intellectual since vanguardism first showed its elitist limitations. It does not mean rejecting all knowledge that is "sacred" or "tried and true," but recognizes a second and secret education, which is both radical and conservative at the very same time: radical because it fights against all forms of indoctrination, conservative because it maintains that which is humanizing. Said may have experienced this schizophrenic education when he recalls, "I always felt that two educations were going on – the conventional education at school and the self-education taking place to satisfy the other self that was excluded" (2001, *PPC*, pp. 281–282). We all find homes, provisional as they are, in disciplines, subject or content areas, and traditions. Teachers are no exception and comfort provides the best company. But the most important problems for the human race to solve will not find their answers in science, literature, or economics, even if these human-made innovations have shepherded us from the dark ages to modernity and beyond. No silver bullet explanations convinced Said that intellectuals were on the precipice of solving world hunger, war, and intolerance. But this fact did not prevent him from isolating problems in the ways we conduct the business of suffering and how to help alleviate it. To Said, this is a sign of the intellectual living amidst the world, an education worth the name.

3
PEDAGOGIES OF EXILE
Learning In and Out of Place

I ain't lost, just wandering.

(Adele, "Hometown Glory")

In many instances, portrayals of exile fall into a familiar narrative. From the Frankfurt School intellectuals who fled Nazi Germany to land in San Diego or Mexico, to Fernando Marcos who was ousted by the historic takeover of Corazon Aquino in the Philippines, exile is usually understood as a political condition borne out of externally imposed departure, usually involving force. But there is another literature on *exile as a modern human condition* resulting from the combination of global migration, war and dispossession, statelessness, economic restructuring, and other disruptions. Said (2000) describes, "Modern Western culture is in large part the work of exiles, émigrés, refugees ... from fascism, communism ...

and expulsion of dissidents" (*Exile*, p. 173). In *Five Faces of Exile*, historian August Espiritu (2005) documents the travels and travails of Filipino intellectuals whose political life or development was complicated by their intricate biographies inside and outside the Philippines. In general, this condition of rootlessness is a process that captures more and more people across the globe as the stable expectation we have grown accustomed to is characterized by the destabilizing experience of millions of people. It is not a life only to be grieved but teaches throngs of people about the permanence of struggle as a way of life. In other words, there is something pedagogical about the exilic condition, not the least of which is the reciprocity between history and those who make knowledge of it.

En route to finding new roots, exiles learn that longtime companions of modern life, such as "home" or "belonging," become tension-filled constructs that can no longer be taken for granted, *even as we long for them*. Indeed, there is something educational about this "pedagogy of exile" that warrants critical conversation in our discipline, if there is something to be gained from a life marked by profound loss for not just an insignificant part of the population. In our turn towards the exile, Edward Said's – and to a lesser extent, Paulo Freire's – writings and reflections are instructive, both as a concrete historical condition and an intellectual position one chooses to take up. The former is familiar to education as immigrants, refugees, or displaced people from war-torn nations enter host countries for opportunity or safety, including their school systems. Although related to the first, the latter is less common in our understanding and the following explication taps into its possibilities of exile as an intellectual choice that educators make in order to disrupt comfortable notions of being and becoming.

Finding Refuge in Exile

The *hermeneutics of exile*, which is simultaneously a "hermeneutics of hope" (Nixon, 2006), is an interpretive choice borne not only out of force and coercion but a deliberate decision to side against certain orthodoxies, normativities, and calcification of power relations. To make his point, Said distinguishes between the "*actual* condition" of exile as opposed to its "*metaphorical* condition" (1994b, *Representations*, p. 52; italics in original). In the U.S., there are groups, from descendants of slaves to multi-generational children of Mexican immigrants, who occupy outsider positions inside society; the most stark example is of course Native Americans, who are exiles on their own land. For Said's own analysis, Palestinian displacement by Israel continues to be a poignant instance of people exiled by exiles. Overall, exile is a mode of existing in the world that reminds the educator of its incompleteness, interconnectedness, and openness.

Seen in this light, exile is the refusal to see social life as a finished product but an evolving history in Vico's sense of a thoroughly human-made endeavor and therefore requires human commitment. Exile then is a "teacher" of precarity in the human condition, what McConaghy (2006) calls "exilic schooling subjectivities" (p. 328). As McConaghy observes, "contests over pedagogy are linked to contests over territory" (p. 329), including its cognitive version as when educators imagine the concept of school as almost always urban or metropolitan, constructing rural students as exiles of official schooling discourse, ruralism as the distant cousin of Orientalism. As such, the framework of exile is a spatial understanding that highlights the centrality of land, geography, and emplacement in the educational process. As a guiding principle for analysis, territory has purchase when educators leverage its utility to describe how power relations move into "new territories," such as the colonization of student cognition, colonialism moving from land takeover to the mind. As well, territoriality means that decolonization moves into different terrains for resistance.

The many forms of exile require assimilating received information about the known world in order to make it hospitable, which is not the same as centric, idealized, or inward iterations of home but rather ex-centric or outward facing towards the experiential world, leading to what Said was fond of calling "worldliness." This state of homelessness should not be taken literally and as one who drives by communities of homeless people on my way to work at UC Berkeley, I want to be clear that people without houses face different challenges from Said who lived a privileged and rarefied life. We are here talking about a political position one chooses, less a state of homelessness but a state of mind where something romantic is lost and grieved, but a sense of humanity is retained, even sharpened. As McConaghy (2006) puts it, "Unhomed, neither here nor back there, the exiled self is located paradoxically, i.e. a paradoxical identity is associated with such displacements and in this process a richer, more complex (teaching) self emerges" (p. 337). The exile is neither merely a subject of excommunication nor exultation, a victim or an Horatio Alger, but that sensibility which represents the human striving to exist in a place while being out of place. It represents a loss of contact with the certainty of earth, where "homecoming is out of the question" (Said, 2000, *Exile*, p. 179). The exile appreciates the comforts of home but understands it is not enough for a full – that is, critical – life.

That established, Said prefers that our current condition be called the "era of the exile." By this, he means that despite the fact that forcible exile may sometimes be accomplished by the end of the barrel of a gun – a condition no one chooses, Freire (1998) reminds us – a generalized life of exile accurately captures the falling away of desires and attachments formerly dominant in traditional modernist thought. Or as Said describes it,

> Modern Western culture is in large part the work of exiles, émigrés, refugees . . . from fascism, communism, expulsion of dissidents. . . . [O]ur age – with its modern warfare, imperialism, and the quasi-theological ambitions of totalitarian rulers – is indeed the age of the refugee, the displaced person, mass immigration.
>
> (2000, *Exile*, pp. 173–174)

As more people are displaced from their houses through expulsion, cities through economic hardships, and nations through war and mass migration, the exilic experience disrupts associations among identity, place, and time previously "guaranteed" by meta-narratives surrounding human and social development. The exile's life runs counter to settler colonial assumptions of putting down roots, often on someone's else's land, and more in line with the process of being uprooted. Rather than settling down, it is the capacity to accommodate being perpetually unsettled as a standard expectation, a dynamic mode of living where sedentariness or stillness becomes an ideological distortion of how real life actually functions for the exile who is always on the move, existentially speaking even when emplaced.

To be clear, the exile's position does not vitiate against *searching* for home and places of belonging. This desire continues in the exile, the colonized, or immigrant. Absent is the romantic attachment of settling down as part of arriving, even a symbol of one's success in having overcome limitations. The exile appreciates being able to put to rest the incessant movement and feeling out of place. But their restlessness reminds them that the dynamism of living does not stop because they have built a life elsewhere because a chosen life is always in the utopic sense of being *nowhere* and *elsewhere* (see Leonardo, 2003b). Exile is precisely a way of living a life that questions its own guarantees. It is not dependent on place although it forms the limit situation in the Freirean sense that place generates the questions that are possible to ask about a life. In all, home is less a place of belonging and more the context that provides the exile the necessary intellectual conditions to exist with others who are also searching for a home. If it is a home, it is an exilic home that provides provisional attachments without their assumed safety.

Said does not mourn the exile's predicament as much as he asserts it as an alternative desire that teaches possibilities about nomadic ways of life, both in terms of actual living conditions and an intellectual choice one makes about how to live a life worth living. That is, the second version of exile involves a certain amount of choice, if by that we mean a deliberate decision to cultivate an intellectual understanding that runs against the grain of accepted traditions and ways of reading socio-educational life. As Said (2000) puts it, conditions of

> exile can produce rancor and regret, as well as a sharpened vision. What has been left behind may either be mourned, or it can be used to provide a different set of lenses . . . using the exile's situation to practice criticism . . . [and] to show that no return to the past is without irony.
>
> (*Exile*, p. xxxv)

Said does not reject feelings of and need for belonging, from the sorts we link to notions of home, to ethnic attachments, or to nationalist movements. His wish was to reread and re-examine, not simply to distort or reject, exile, but ultimately forge a "radical exilic vision" (Said, 2000, *Exile*, p. xxxiv).

We might surmise that the verb "to belong" is a double-edged sword to suggest, on the one hand, feelings of community and, on the other hand, a form of possession, such that both slaves and the colonies were once their masters' property. Said does not provide us with convenient notions of ownership that elide power relations in exchange for an innocence that forgets what Raymond Williams (1977), an intellectual whom Said admired, calls "structures of feeling." In his lifetime for example, Said fought for Palestinian rights to a "homeland," bringing him both celebrity status and attracting a politics of derision. Likewise, he had a clear sense of his own Palestinian identity (however unordinary it was) and his attachment to it. But he was less sanguine about the prospects of Palestinian *independence* and *sovereignty*, which, for him, were only steps along the way to the more significant task of *liberation*. For Said, the exile's negative experience with a certain "possessive investment" (Lipsitz's phrase, 1998) in an essentialized identity provides a cautionary tale about the perils of feeling a sense of belonging with one's socially constructed self. As Hugo of St. Victor says profoundly, "The man who finds his homeland sweet is still a tender beginner . . . but he is perfect to whom the entire world is as a foreign land" (as quoted by Said, 2000, *Exile*, p. 185). Indigenous people from North to South America, Australia, and the Pacific Islands know the irony of being treated as foreigners on their own land through settler colonialism through which the concept of nation was forcefully introduced. Exiles at home, native peoples were once creatures of the world, now reduced to second-class citizens of an imposed nation.

Compare the exile with the colonizer who wants to make the whole world his home in his own image. The exile's development, which is based on solitude, is at cross-purposes with nationalism and other affinities, which are based on group mentality. Although an unyielding critic of colonialism and empire, Said found nationalist counter-movements against power necessary but ultimately insufficient projects. As Said understands it, "Nationalism is the philosophy of identity made into a collectively organized passion" (2000, *Exile*, p. 402), which is a necessary first step for the margins but degrades when it focuses on one's or "*our own* separateness" (p. 403; italics in original). Insofar as it is necessary, "All nationalisms in their early stages develop from a condition of estrangement" (Said, 2000, *Exile*, p. 176). By contrast, the exile's solitude does not equate with privacy but rather with a fierce humanism that values independent, self-critical thought while capable of admitting completion through an other who is not a threat but a complement of the self.

The Exile's Personality

The exile is a product of historical development. To the extent that they exhibit a personality, Said (2000) reminds us that it is cobbled from the contradictory, heterogeneous, and worldly situation of the exile to which they have been condemned (*Exile*, p. xv). Said reminds us that exiles are prone to willfulness, exaggeration, and overstatement, which reflect the felt severity of their condition. On occasion, they are not beyond a certain fetish of exile as a sense of "narcissistic masochism," "petulant cynicism," "querulous lovelessness" (2000, *Exile*, p. 183). In all, the exile is condemned to history much like Merleau-Ponty (1963) once declared humans are creatures condemned to meaning, whose phenomenology insists that humans exist in the world before they can think about it. That is, any systematic study of the exile's personality takes as its beginning the history that makes its suffering possible but also that which makes it meaningful. Extending Dewey's (1938) thoughts on experience, Said makes visible the human traffic that makes culture possible at a global level, a perpetual state of movement that offers an alternative to the western preference for stillness and the immovable mover. Said affirms the immediacy of direct experience and abstract theory fails when it moves us away from experience more and more, escaping from it.

As a literary and comparatist scholar, Said insists that weighty events in history, like imperialism and colonialism, enter literature and language. Here, we note Said's weariness about linguistic idealism because he insists that language refers to real historical experience rather than being self-referential, language qua language. For this reason, great novels, like Conrad's *Heart of Darkness*, are not monuments by artists as lone writers but instead are expressions of authors' inimitable personalities produced by their concrete material conditions. In Conrad's instance, Said's admiration for the Polish exile shines through even as Said lambasts him for his colonial gaze and excesses concerning Africa. Even Kipling's *Kim*, a colonizer's guide to India, receives praise from Said because of its symptomatic reading of a settler's self-account of colonialism. Conrad's *Nostromo* is similar for its unveiling of coloniality in South America. Finally, Austen's novels have stood the test of time partly for their naked portrayal of colonial power relations and literature's complicity with the history that interpellates them, even if the *Pride and Prejudice* author did not intend it. Contrary to the urge simply to reject these problematic texts, Said values them for their ambivalences, an apt task for a hermeneutics of exile. Said reserves his greatest praise for the German Jewish philologist, Auerbach, whose tome *Mimesis*v was published in 1953 during his exile in Istanbul, culling through the minimalist archives of western culture available to him, literally and figuratively. *Mimesis*, which Said (2004) calls "an exile's book" (*HDC*, p. 97) – not unlike Said's own *Culture and Imperialism* – represents the confirmation of Vico's *The New Science* (1984), which, for Said, inaugurates secularism's ability to know only what humans have themselves created: mainly culture. Said's Vician appreciation shines through when he writes,

> For in its essence the intellectual life . . . is about the freedom to be critical: criticism is intellectual life and . . . its spirit is intellectual and critical, and neither reverential nor patriotic. One of the great lessons of the critical spirit is that human life and history are secular – that is, actually constructed and reproduced by men and women.
>
> (2000, *Exile*, p. 397)

With Said, these authors share the exile's personality, which is constantly at odds with the conditions of its own making. Thus, the "starting point of any philosophical enterprise is man's [sic] own life" (Said, 2000, *Exile*, p. 2). Taken too literally, Vico's insight will not make complete sense since astronomers are able to understand the structure of the universe, which humans did not in fact create. Vico, and therefore Said by association, suggests that humans can only understand what they themselves have created in terms of social life and history. And if the universe has a history since the Big Bang that astronomers consider the holy grail and exists just outside the ability of scientific instruments to detect, it is a different history with which Said is concerned. For Said, human traffic, not asteroids, constitutes the cultural history he interprets from the position of the exile. It is there where the "conflict of interpretations" (Ricoeur, 2007) begins. Despite debates among physicists as to whether or not the asteroid belt resulted from a planet or satellite disintegrating in the orbit between Mars and Jupiter, humanistic exegesis requires engaging with human will and agency in a way that responds differently from rocks, insights from new materialism notwithstanding.

Like Freire, the philosopher of education who wandered the world for 16 years after the military coup in Brazil, Said confirms the exile's restless personality. Exilic living represents a radical break with everyday life, looking for an alternative, while living both. It is different from Swift's example of "tragic restlessness," who finds little in social life in which to pleasure, so he attacks it all (Said, 1983, *WTC*, p. 89)! As Freire advises, there is a break with your past brought about by exile but "you must not make the break any greater than it is" (1998, p. 197). It is a form of schizophrenia of the order that Deleuze and Guattari (1983) spoke about in *Anti-Oedipus*, or the experience of simultaneity, of metaphoric schizophrenia rather than its clinical version. Anathema to the colonial trope of "settlement," exile is fundamentally an unsettling experience, an almost paranoid life of looking forward while watching your back. In terms of bigotry, you desire to reverse racism! (a declarative, according to Roediger, 1994), while avoiding forms of reverse chauvinism, such as Orientalism's opposite found in Occidentalism, or demonization of everything Europe as a false answer to the disparagement of everything non-western. This is not unlike Appiah's (1990) distinction between intrinsic and extrinsic racism, the former an ideology that asserts an in-group's essential sameness, the latter imposing one's norms on an out-group. The first, which finds its expression in most forms of nationalism (including during decolonization, see Fanon, 2005), is distinguishable in its consequences within the relations of force from the second for which Nazism and Apartheid are modern examples. An exile desires home without putting down roots in an attempt to make someone else's home their own, literally and figuratively.

Exiles live in a perpetually jealous state. They sense that nothing is certain, stuck between the insecurity of possibly having your possessions (including memories) taken away from you yet not wanting to share those same possessions because of a heightened sense of difference from non-exiles. But neither is the exile to be envied; it would be like envying the slave who sees the nature of oppression more accurately than the master. Neither the slave nor exile seems to need this kind of recognition. For the exile's part, it may be a kind of paternalism that we would be better off avoiding. The exile loses a sense of contact with the certainty of the earth on which non-exiles rely, because for the exile "homecoming is out of the question" (Said, 2000, *Exile*, p. 179; see also He, 2010). As a result, nothing is religious or sacred and the "exile is irremediably secular and unbearably historical," (Said, 2000, *Exile*, p. 174) in Vico's sense. Here, "religious" is not only a term that designates the institutionalization of beliefs in certain gods, but, as it concerns intellectual life, religious is the process of canonizing sacred texts, forms of knowledge, and ways of thinking. Often, canons are flanked by cannons, Kant with cant when it regards non-western literature. The exile has little patience for this kind of elevation of what Matthew Arnold (1867) once described as "Culture," or the best that a society produces. He prefers sensibilities for the contrapuntal, like two independent melodies in music that weave in and out of each other.

Home, Time and Place, and Development of the Exile

If there is a home for the exile, it is to be found in writing: the only home, as Adorno once said. But even this home is still provisional. It was this way for James Joyce, the Irish author who left his beloved Ireland in order to capture it through writing, choosing exile as a way to achieve clarity about the place he called home precisely by being out of place. To this list, we may add expatriates who voluntarily live in other countries, such as Ernest Hemingway and F. Scott Fitzgerald. In Said's (1999) memoir, *Out of Place*, we receive a similar portrait of this artist as a young man. In fact, it is no small matter that he calls his own book, *Culture and Imperialism*, an "exile's book" (1994a, p. xxvi).

There are obvious differences between the two varieties of exile, perhaps the defining factor being the presence of overt force. Said's suggestion is that one can *choose to side with the exile* even if coercion is absent. This is not to say that we should pretend to be exiles in the literal sense if in fact we are not so but to stand next, with, or adjacent to the exile. By comparison, the concept of the refugee is a modern, political stigma, whereas exile as a form of banishment is accompanied by solitude, even spirituality. When asked by Ari Shavit during an interview, "Are you a refugee?", Said answers, "No, the term refugee has a very specific meaning for me. That is to say, poor health, social misery, loss and dislocation. That does not apply to me. In that sense, I'm not a refugee. But I feel I have no place. I'm cut off from my origins. I live in exile. I am exiled" (2001, *PPC*, p. 456). The former is an externally and internationally imposed classification, often bureaucratic for purposes of social services and state administration, whereas the latter in the sense promoted here is internally defined and chosen. This is not a nod to the liberal, modern subject's ability to establish sovereignty over discourses that vie for their subjectivity but provides an alternative reading of the exile that goes against the grain of current political discourses of certainty and determinism.

As intellectuals from Marx, who sided politically with the working class despite being existentially "outside" it, to Memmi, who benefited from colonialism as a Tunisian Jew but stood with the colonized, it is possible to take the position of the other without being the other in all instances. Exile is not a privilege but an alternative, not a matter of simple choice, and "provided that the exile refuses to sit on the sidelines nursing a wound, there are things to be learned: he or she must cultivate a scrupulous (not indulgent or sulky) subjectivity" (Said, 2000, *Exile*, p. 184; cf. Freire, 1998). In a sense, the exile finds home within a condition of homelessness because they belong to the world rather than to a race, culture, or nation. As a form of possession, belonging is Janus-faced and Merleau-Ponty reminds us in *Phenomenology of Perception* that "the world is not what I think, but what I live through . . . I am in communication with it, but I do not possess it" (as cited by Said, 2000, *Exile*, p. 5). In short, this move represents a desire against propertizing the yearning for belongingness, of turning it into a commodity form, that is, a private property. But with this loss of possessiveness comes a sharper vision if the exile is sensitive to their and others' histories, their and others' struggles. Said knows better than to romanticize homelessness as such, but argues instead that marginality and homelessness are not to be glorified but stamped out.

Exiles look on with resentment at non-exiles, those who presume to belong. If non-exiles feel a sense of centeredness, exiles are eccentrics who insist on their difference, state of being orphaned, and on some level enjoyment in asserting their right to refuse to belong. Living a "borrowed life" (p. 196), as Freire (1998) once put it, exiles exist in a discontinuous state of being, that is, cut off from one's origins, land, and past. They long to belong but never quite find it, never quite consummate it, stumbling forward out of sync with both place and time. They suffer a historical disjuncture with spatial relations because they do not have constant reminders of the place they once inhabited. They do not have the luxury of revisiting their childhood house, school, or playground, which haunt them like ghosts, and not only in the sense of a frightful apparition. The meandering roads do not take them to their former destinations. They remember with fondness yet frustration glimmers of their previous selves, random scenes of a life lived elsewhere, which visit them in fits and starts: a street here, a store there, an insignificant exchange in a friend's house, a gesture. Said (2000) writes, "[W]hat is true of all exile is not that home and love of home are lost, but that loss is inherent in the very existence of both" (*Exile*, p. 185). The exile does not enjoy the comparative spatial continuity more typical of non-exile existence.

In an essay that appeared in *The World, the Text, and the Critic* (1983), "Traveling Theory" and later, "Traveling Theory Reconsidered" in *Reflections on Exile* (2000), Said guides our sensibility for movement – against the hegemony of permanence and fixity – by affirming the intellectual nomad. He suggests this restless portrait,

> The image of the traveler depends not on power but on motion, on a willingness to go into different worlds, use different idioms, and understand a variety of disguises, masks, and rhetorics. Travelers

> must suspend the claim of customary routine in order to live in new rhythms and rituals. Most of all, and most unlike the potentate who must guard only one place and defend its frontiers, the traveler *crosses over*, traverses territory, and abandons fixed positions, all the time.
>
> (2000, *Exile*, p. 404; italics in original)

The exile's spatial relation is both particular or specific, such that their unique trajectory is not replicable, but is also universal in that they bear the human mark of displacement and dislocation that bonds them to others. Or as La Paperson (aka Wayne Yang) (2010) ironically points out, the ghetto is not a location but precisely a dislocation. Like a dislocated shoulder, whereby the joint is out of place, we register a pain. And when the exile lacks alignment with official culture (or "home culture"), a similar but emotional anguish results from being disjointed. The traveler is Said's preferred trope, which is different from the explorer or discoverer, these last characters obviously carrying ideological baggage for Said. In his sense, travelers do not partake in discovering a strange land and people to annunciate their existence by making them visible or writing them into history. Travelers enable their environment to make them strange(rs) to themselves. This self-estrangement is critical to their unfolding or becoming, over and again, to become different from themselves, to become something else in the process, to be elsewhere even as they stand somewhere.

Temporally, exiles suffer a historical break in their personal (no longer just individual) continuum. They are not unlike an immigrant whose life almost begins anew in a host country but feels cheated out of the years they lived in their birth land. I say "almost" because an exile's history is more akin to quantum space and time, which does not follow a linear progression. For example, previously an immigrant child at 10 years old, the adult version at 40 feels chronologically 30, feeling younger than a comparably aged native citizen yet also older because of an exaggerated sense of migration's cruelties. Research tells us that immigrant children mature more quickly in certain respects when they are forced to become intermediaries or translators between schools and their parents, culturally and linguistically (see Portes & Rumbaut, 2001). This role reversal between children as caretakers of adults causes undue stress that immigrant youth, still immature in other respects, experience and do not always know how to explain to themselves, let alone to others. They are adultified in the process, something that Ann Ferguson (2001) also noticed in her studies of Black boys' institutional relation with schools. Or to use an oft-used adult tactic, when exiles act out they are put in time out because they are out of time. In the case of Black boys and men, who did not choose a life of exile, the phrase "little man" for the former and the well-known term of derision, "boy," for the latter, confirm that they are out of step with standard, colonial-racial, time. Both never seem to arrive at the appropriate developmental, human stage because, as Fanon (2008) reminds us in *Black Skin, White Masks*, Blacks of any age exist in the temporality of non-being.

In fact, to achieve the status of being (i.e., human) is to be a creature of time. For Fanon, the fact of blackness sequesters Black subjects in a spacetime that combines Einstein's physics with a general theory of Blacks' racial relativity to whiteness, something that Du Bois (1989) was well aware of in the U.S. context. Exiles follow a different calendar, a divergent order of things, an alter/native way of being. They are truly creatures of the future because looking back is filled with contradictions and ironies about desires for a bountiful past. They are forward looking rather than backward longing. Said admits, "Exile is sometimes better than staying behind or not getting out: but only sometimes" (2000, *Exile*, p. 178). For the exile, "the very act of doing criticism entails a commitment to the future" (Said, 2000, *Exile*, p. 167). That established, they are out of sync only if we recognize that both space and time are warped by the gravity of race, racism, and whiteness, or what William Appleman Williams calls "empire as a way of life" (cited by Said, 2000, *Exile*, p. 305). CPT is only one consequence of this colonial clock.

To live in historical time, exiles become painfully aware that they cannot afford romantic or wishful thinking. This is loss of a certain innocence, even more cruel for a child, whom education's disciplinary roots once sentimentalized. With respect to colonialism's effects on the child, the literature is inadequate, so much of the attention falling on its destruction of adult men and women. In the article "Fanon's Other Children," Burman (2017) considers the havoc that the psycho-existential complex of colonialism wreaks on the child whose arrested development is simultaneously sped up, becoming adult minds in children's bodies. In other instances, colonialism infantilizes native adults, treating them as out of sync with time, or children's minds in adult bodies. The violence they witness or experience is a repressed phenomenon that is not well understood, which may be an argument for a stolen childhood under the thumb of colonialism. It would be difficult to assimilate such an experience with many extant works on childhood development in educational scholarship. It is plain enough to see that children are different from adults, but less is known about the effects of colonialism as a creator of the "child," and more broadly childhood as a discrete stage of life within colonialism.

PEDAGOGIES OF EXILE   73

With respect to the colonizer's children, Fanon gives us at least a little more information, such as when a White child describes fears about being eaten by a Black man in *Black Skin, White Masks*. The monstrosity of blackness invented by colonialism reaches its spectacular image in the colonizer child's Freudian nightmare. Fanon's famous interpellative sentence, "Look, a Negro!", encapsulates the colonial gaze, all the way down to White children. The irony should be clear that the ravages of colonialism is able to create savages, if not cannibals, out of the colonized although its cruelties would be judged uncivilized by the archives of history. If Fanon famously argued that the colonized are actional even in their dreams – jumping and running as it were – and decolonization continues during slumber, it would seem that the colonizer are dystopic in their waking moments. Although both scenarios involve children, whereby the colonized child loses innocence and the colonizer child feigns it, they are children of different orders, or if we want to use Fanon's terminology, zones of child being and non-being. We might go so far as to say that whereas the colonizer child maintains the privilege of being a child, the colonized child is not a child at all but an adult simulacram and by extension the colonized adult is a child simulacram.

More well known is Fanon's metaphorical use of time, often unwittingly disableist. Burman excavates Fanon's use of metaphor to expose his teleological language involving the developmental relation between time, the child, and adulthood. It is hardly a surprise to see that Fanon, a self-proclaimed rationalist, is ensnared by the usual developmental approach that conceives of child stages as immature, zealous, and to be transcended. Through passages taken from *Black Skin, White Masks* and *The Wretched of the Earth*, Burman finds Fanon's bias against the "young bourgeoisie" and "young nation" after the expulsion of the colonizer as depictions of the lifecourse projected onto the budding decolonization movement. This is Fanon's recapitulation of ageism into his analysis, a disabling framework that the civilized colonizer (read: mature, modern) once used against the backward colonized (read: immature, ancient). Burman argues that Fanon does even more; the Martinican also grafts childhood traits onto the colonizer, or Europe/ans, as basically having a sleeping rationality that needs to be awakened, abruptly wrestling them from their fairy tale existence, not unlike existence in Plato's proverbial cave.

One senses that Althusser's (1971) use of the "epistemological break" to distinguish between the young, early, or anthropological Marx and the more mature, scientific Marx (i.e., the properly "Marxist" Marx) applies to Fanon's relatively short life and career. *Black Skin* is unapologetically humanist (even as it disavows European humanism), existential (critiques of his friend Sartre notwithstanding), and emotion-filled (despite distrusting fervor), perhaps even personal (we are reminded of his relationship with Jolie, per chapters two and three on interracial coupling). On the other hand, *Wretched* is programmatic, detached, and, one might argue, scientific. If there is a case to be made of a "young Fanon" in *Black Skin*, there is evidence of a "mature Fanon" in *Wretched*. As insidious as this may sound in light of Eurocentric colonial temporality, Fanon did not reject a certain decolonial appropriation of linearity and teleology.

For the child exile, growing up is a hasty process. We note this happening in the immigrant's experience, or today's Black boy traversing city streets in Oakland, Ferguson, or Sacramento. Already out of time, he'd better not find himself out of place, which could turn fatal. Rousseau's (1979) Emile was taught to be carefree of the world's worries, whereas the exile is too much **of** this world. The luxury of childhood time is violated as part of the death drive. After all, *schole* (the root word for "school") is Greek for "leisure," which seems to run in the opposite direction of the word "curriculum," the Latin word for "race course" (Kliebard, 2004). Later as adults, exiles recognize the "[t]ension between roots in new environment, denial of origins. . . . The history and culture of their environment have not stood still waiting for them!" (Freire, 1998, p. 210). It is not uncommon for exiles to speak of a "return" to some lost homeland only to be rudely awakened by the brutal fact that time did not sit idly waiting for their rendezvous with history. Freire confronts this dynamic when he faces a new Brazil upon his return from Guinea-Bissau, Geneva's Council of Churches, and other stops during his period of exile. The dangers of romanticizing home and place are a constitutive part of the hermeneutics of exile where an accurate interpretation of time is crucial.

We see this dynamic on display when the parents in the movie, "East is East," are mocked by their children, indeed by their own memories of their homeland, Pakistan. The father longs for a Pakistan of previous decades, idealized beyond its reality, removing lived tensions from its history. To him, Pakistan is frozen in time and he remembered it in the condition when he walked away from it; of course, even this is a form of mystification since his representation of life in Pakistan is likely better, in the romantic sense, than it actual was. This mistake in attribution does not make him deplorable but nostalgia is part and parcel of exile. His children, exiles in their own right, already live in their own time and place as young Pakistanis in the U.K., without recourse to an originary attachment to Pakistan. They do not claim an essential Pakistani status but want the right merely to be. Meanwhile, their father adopt a super-Pakistani identity, literally "full of himself."

For his own part, Said returns to his childhood house in occupied Palestine only to find that a Christian organization has put down roots there. This may serve as an unintentional and even sardonic reminder of Said's family's minority status as Christians in the once Muslim-majority nation. Crestfallen, Said agrees with Freire (1998) who admits,

> Exiles are preparing themselves to return home without arrogance. They return without believing that their environment owes them something for the mere fact of their having been in exile. They return without claiming to be superior to those who remained.
>
> (p. 210)

Said was a public supporter of the Palestinians' "rights to return" to former Palestine, but he was clear of this repatriation's ironies. Until his death, he insisted on a two-state solution between Israel and Palestine, yearning for the Palestinians' rightful place but refusing to de-home Jews any further. Exiles are human beings out of place with an acute sense that they are running out of time. But more unlucky are they who convince themselves that home is where the heart is, a place of belonging and arrival.

White Teachers and Pedagogies of Exile

If we keep in mind that as a profession, teaching is populated mostly by White teachers, it would be difficult to avoid racial considerations in both the theory and practice of education. Further, if we keep in mind that teachers are not only majority White but overwhelmingly women, there is a gendered racial specificity to teaching as well (see Leonardo & Boas, 2013). One of the challenges we face as a discipline is the growing population of students of color and a steady stream of White female teachers. The year 2050 has been signaled as a relevant marker predicting the majority of school-going children coming from families of color. I do not wish to inflect this point with what I call a "demographic threat" or "populational ultimatum," but it is a familiar refrain for anyone concerned with making teaching relevant to students. For the purposes of this chapter, what lessons are gained from Said's thoughts and insights on exile if we apply it to the whiteness of teaching, which often defaults to the teaching of whiteness to many kids of color? In this last section, I appropriate Said's general framework – as well as Freire's, in some cases – for the analytics of a pedagogy of exile. In short, what does it mean for White teachers to take the position of the exile?

In a 1989 conversation with Antonio Faundez in the book *Learning to Question*, which was later collected in the edited volume *The Paulo Freire Reader*, Freire (1998) reflects on his time away from Brazil. He would have been warranted if he confessed feeling the sting of injustice and even martyrdom. Freire nevertheless concludes, "It is a mistake to think of exile in purely negative terms. It can also become a deeply enriching, deeply creative experience if, in the fight for survival, we exiles achieve a minimum of physical comfort" (1998, p. 190). Separately and independent of one another, Said and Freire wrote about the existential condition of exile they experienced during the 1970s. In their writings, we learn the lessons about what it means to unbelong, to dehome, and to be out of place. But to White teachers, what would it mean to encourage them to go into exile when they feel right at home or in place? Indeed, self-selecting exile in order to make their world both strange and familiar, neither Said nor Freire's work suggests that choosing this white apostasy promotes self-hatred but rather self-understanding. On the contrary, White exile familiarizes teachers with what they otherwise have lacked critical knowledge about: mainly, that being White is not just another racial identity, just another home. It is special, but perhaps not in the way that Whites would prefer or have been taught to think about the exceptionality of whiteness. From Christine Sleeter (1993) to Gary Howard (2006), we learn that White teachers woefully lack appreciation of their racial conditioning; it goes to reason that participating in critical discussions about whiteness produces a strange and awkward feeling for many Whites. Familiarizing themselves with what they have become as a result of racialization is a prelude to making whiteness strange: mainly, that having white skin (in the sense of Weber's ideal types) should matter no more than having big feet (see Ignatiev & Garvey, 1996).

Through the hermeneutics of exile, White teachers become critical travelers, in Said's sense, and not as explorers and discoverers as such. They journey into the heart of whiteness, something they are rarely encouraged to do and which they have avoided. But they perform this act of exile, at the same time an act of disobedience, in order then to objectify whiteness for study, for scrutiny, in order to increase self-understanding. As Freire (1998) recalls,

> It was by passing through all these different parts of the world as an exile that I came to understand my own country better. It was by seeing it from a distance, it was by standing back from it, that I came to understand myself better. It was by being confronted with another self that I discovered more easily my own identity.
>
> (p. 199)

As part of revealing the self to oneself, auto-estrangement proceeds in order not just to know thyself, as Socrates once suggested, but to know thyself differently. By facing himself as an other through the process of exile, Freire was able to understand himself better. Likewise, White teachers stand to comprehend their identity better by familiarizing themselves with whiteness and then defamiliarizing it, that is, by choosing exile. Only then does whiteness become something foreign and therefore a source of true insight rather than the folk knowledge that passes as whiteness.

By objectifying whiteness under study, White teachers understand their uniqueness as racial beings. They come to terms with their racialized conditioning, which is not of their own personal making but nonetheless requires their consent. Exile provides White teachers a sense of humility about their insertion into racial history, which becomes a more realistic appraisal of their involvement in racism, even if it is through complicity rather than active domination of people of color. It opens rather than closes off culture, cultural interaction, even cultural accomplishments when they are not elevated over and against other groups' achievements. As Freire (1998) recounts, "I discovered how strong the distinctive marks of our culture are, but how much stronger they become if we don't treat them as absolutes" (p. 208). Consistent with the politics of recognition, White teacher exiles learn to appreciate the specificity of their experience while respecting others' particularity. In the process, they fulfill their singularity such that no other is like them, while also participating in the universality of the human experience. They recognize that "[e]xiles become subjects in the learning process . . . accepting critically their situation as exiles" (Freire, 1998, p. 209). As they leave the comforts of whiteness, they realize that walking *away* from something also means walking *towards* something else, that leaving behind their home means finding another. It is registered as a loss but white loss is not like other losses, like when children of color suffer deculturalization in schools (Spring, 2000; Valenzuela, 1999). White exiles prepare for breaks in their family relations, friendships, intimate others, and self-understanding, whose destabilizing effects should not be underestimated or minimized. That said, what Whites gain by accepting the negativity of exile releases them from an existential burden (different from Kipling's "White Man's Burden") in exchange for connection over separation, community over segregation, and conviviality over alienation. It leads them finally to appreciate what it really means to be socially White.

For White teachers, exile represents a break. It does not reach the proportions of what Ignatiev and Garvey (1996) encourage when they ask Whites to break apart the "White club" in order to dissolve or abolish it. Not yet. Rather, for the exile the break is about disrupting routines and habits by replacing them with new ones. It is closer to the "epistemological break" (Althusser, 1976) whereby the social world is retheorized and comes into focus, more or less scientifically. As Freire (1998) says,

> Exile is not simply a break at the epistemological, emotional, affective, intellectual, or even political levels: it is also a break in your daily life, which is made up of gestures, words, loving human relationships . . . to become literate at the level of being.
>
> (pp. 206–207)

So much of being White, that is, *White being*, is about the everydayness of the taken-for-granted aspects of belonging. De-routinizing whiteness disrupts the body's habituations, what Bonilla-Silva, Goar, and Embrick (2006) call the "White habitus," to expose White assumptions about knowledge worth learning, minds worth cultivating, and, finally, a life worth living.

Choosing exile represents a rupture in White teacher consciousness. It is experienced no less than a puncture in their existence through space and time: space, because they must deterritorialize what they thought belonged only to them; time, because they must reorient themselves to a different rhythm of life that is forward looking. Said (2000) writes, "Exile is sometimes better than staying behind or not getting out: but only sometimes" (*Exile*, p. 178). Whites will find themselves restless and fractured, with an "ambiguous feeling of freedom, on one hand . . . and on the other of having suffered a tragic break in [their] history" (Freire, 1998, p. 197), which puts them closer to what many people of color already experience through double-consciousness (Du Bois, 1989), without going as far as suggesting that White double-consciousness exists as a structural possibility (Leonardo, 2013; cf. Yancy, 2012; Alcoff, 2015; Sider, 2019). The specificity of double-consciousness for Blacks results from a *power imposition* whereby they exist as black *within* a white world that necessitates reckoning, structurally speaking, with white regard for the black. There may be at least two distortions of blackness here, primarily by the white imagination and secondarily the compromised black imagination for which authenticity is elusive under conditions of white power. No comparable process exists for Whites, for whom blackness, as Fanon (2008) reminds us, exercises no ontological resistance, as if Blacks were "invisible men [sic]" to Whites (Ellison, 1952). To this, Fanon adds a third consciousness based on the Black body, who observes,

> In the train, it was a question of being aware of my body, no longer in the third person but in triple. In the train, instead of one seat, they

left me two or three. . . . I was responsible not only for my body but also my race and my ancestors.

(2008, p. 92)

From the modern and united subject to Du Bois' twoness, we arrive at Fanon's hermeneutics of black threeness, or a corporeal materialist theory of race. This established, we may go so far as to suggest that, as exiles, Whites begin to understand the "ambiguity of [their] being and not being" (Freire, 1998, p. 190) and with respect to race, distinguish what is real and not real about a racialized social life (Leonardo, 2005). They learn to be schizoid subjects who simultaneously remember and forget they are White: remember, in order to understand the power of being White; forget, in order to assert their general humanity among a sea of humans.

White re-birth cannot be accomplished through colorblindness, which is synonymous with perishing in race rather than emerging from it. Freire (1998) observes, "Either we learn to surmount the negativity caused by the break with the past, so as to discover and seize the opportunities presented by the new environment, or else we perish in exile" (p. 197). Whereas White exile begins with a negation, it becomes, as Marx might put it, a negation of the negation. In Freire's words, exile is "a break which has to be destroyed in order to be transcended, and this fresh break has to be transcended by another" (p. 212). In order to be productive, White exile turns the break into an opportunity to reflect on what the White subject has accepted, often without question, to which they no longer consent. It leads to what Freire and Faundez (1989) call "learning to question" or "existence itself as an act of questioning" (Freire, 1998, p. 227), the prerequisite of any knowledge that contributes to a full life, and not in the sense that it is comparatively fuller by virtue of what one can deny another. The pedagogy of exile is a race-conscious cognition even as it strides for a radical humanism, of which one premise resides in questioning what race has made of us, to which we no longer consent. Whites' place in that project is indeed specific, in fact distinct, but it is connected "with a freight of urgency" (Said, 2000, *Exile*, p. xxi) to the plight of people of color who have suffered its vestiges for hundreds of years and which lives on through sheer and daily repetition of the injury known as race.

4
EDUCATIONAL CRITICISM AND CONTRAPUNTAL ANALYSIS

> In music, force is not power, something that many of the world's political leaders do not perceive. The difference between power and force is equivalent to the difference between volume and intensity in music. When one speaks with a musician and says to him, "You are not playing intensely enough," his first reaction is to play louder. And it is exactly the opposite: the lower the volume, the greater the need for intensity, and the greater the volume, the greater need for a calm force in the sound.
>
> (Barenboim, 2005, "Maestro")

In 1976, Elliot Eisner proposed a research program he called "educational criticism" in the *Journal of Aesthetic Education*. In it, he compared criticism to connoisseurship, where the first is about disclosure, its success proportional to its ability to illuminate, and the second, about appreciation. Another differentiating feature is that connoisseurship is private whereas criticism is public and requires connoisseurship but connoisseurship does not necessitate facility with criticism. In the mid-1970s, he noted that the discipline of education did not promote criticism as a branch of study, citing as his evidence,

> We do not have, for example, journals of educational criticism or critical theory. We do not have programs in universities that prepare educational critics. We do not have a tradition of thought dealing with the formal, systematic, scholarly study and practice of educational criticism.
>
> (Eisner, 1976, p. 141)

To Eisner, educational criticism consists of a descriptive, interpretive, and evaluative function, all of which leads to the critic's ability to adumbrate the educational value of insights gained from empirical investigation as they distill the essence of a context, like a chef boils away a concoction to reveal the flavorful reduction. Not unlike Said, Eisner notes that the

> task of the critic is not simply one of being a neutral observer (an impossible position in any case), nor is it one of disinterested interpretation. The critic uses what he or she sees and interprets in order to arrive at some conclusions about the character of educational practice and to its improvement.
>
> (p. 146)

As an illuminating practice, criticism's task is the "reeducation of perception" (p. 148), which is possible only with the benefit of good and valid criticism, eventually leading to "a more catholic sense of possibility" (p. 149).

Over 40 years later, the educational discipline still does not embrace a new specialization under the title of "criticism." The most convenient evidence for this arid field rests on the non-existent job calls for an "educational critic" in a sea of positions found in "teacher education," "measurement," or "educational psychology." Whereas a graduate student of literature would likely run into calls for a tenure track position in "literary criticism," no parallel job offering exists for an education scholar. There are approximations but they are not equivalent in the eyes and standards of the discipline. Attempts to revive interest in criticism notwithstanding (Leonardo, 2004, 2016b; Uhrmacher, Moroye, & Flinders, 2017), it appears that whereas in allied disciplines, literary, art, or philosophical criticism survives or thrives, educational critics would be wise to consider other ways to market ourselves. On the other hand, as a research agenda, criticism has steadily grown as an industry and educational scholars busy themselves outlining what criticality means, present author included. Since at least the English translation of Paulo Freire's (1993) *Pedagogy of the Oppressed* and Aronowitz and Giroux's (1985) innovation that goes by the name of Critical Pedagogy, criticism has found a provisional home in education. That is, while critics in education should not hold their breath for a job, the work is being done.

Although criticism in education abounds, often "blamed" on Critical Pedagogy (e.g., see Giroux, 1983; McLaren, 2015), it is ostensibly the case that the discipline has yet to own that specialization. Not quite the red-headed stepchild, neither is Crit Ped the favored child, which has to do with commonsense or uncritical understandings of criticism. As a result, the function and role of criticism is only beginning to make inroads in the discipline despite decades of Dewey's (1916, 1938) powerful treatises on schooling; education scholars are more comfortable regarding his work as examples of philosophy rather than criticism. In general, criticism is pigeonholed as a practice for those negative nabobs who insist on complaining about education's woes rather than building a constructive alternative. Consequently, educational criticism receives short shrift, a victim of caricature and emptied of character.

Building Educational Criticism

In this last chapter, I want to argue that, like philological criticism, art criticism, or film criticism, educational criticism is a rich tapestry or collection of insights only loosely answering to that nickname. Although arguing for a new specialization in education risks the professionalization that Said (*Representations*, 1994b) warns intellectuals against, the discipline would benefit from developing educational criticism as a bona fide area with its own discursive community, institutional supports, and traditions. And yes . . . a job would be nice too. For instance, in 1998, I accepted an assistant professorship at the University of St. Thomas, Minnesota in a fledgling doctoral program in Critical Pedagogy, the only one of its kind during and since that time, to my knowledge. The program closed roughly ten years later. On another occasion, I recall a job position at Montclair State University, New Jersey carrying the descriptor "critical pedagogy." There are others I have missed, for sure. Such was the influence of Paulo Freire's *Pedagogy of the Oppressed* and Giroux's success at building the specialization of Critical Pedagogy in the U.S. These days, a young academic in the U.S. is more likely to compete for a job with the descriptor "Critical Race Theory" rather than "Critical Pedagogy" attached to it. Since Ladson-Billings and Tate's (1995)

Teachers College Record essay that launched a thousand books, CRT has enjoyed a burgeoning presence in the field.

Neither of these examples equates with the establishment of a broader engagement with educational criticism. They are discipline-changing innovations and have recruited many scholars to their cause, myself included. But their reach, to my own chagrin, remains confined, sometimes boxed-in, in the discipline. With respect to CRT, the implicit assumption is that race and racism are non-negotiables so research unrelated to race will be hard-pressed to find an audience in CRT. On the other matter, Critical Pedagogy's future appears uncertain. With Freire's passing and Kincheloe's untimely death, Giroux's exit from the U.S. scene to head north to Canada with a new office in the Department of English and Cultural Studies, and McLaren and Scatamburlo D'Annibale's (2005) pronouncement that Critical Pedagogy has outrun its usefulness as a result of excessive theorizing from a post-structural or identity politics perspective, third generation Crit Peddlers may become institutionally homeless, and not necessarily in the vein of Said's exile.

Yet with the planetary instabilities that wreak havoc in every corner of the globe, educational criticism is needed now more than ever. Critical educational policy analysis (e.g., from Stephen Ball and Dave Gillborn in the U.K.; Kal Gulson, Fazal Rizvi, and Bob Lingard in Australia; and Pauline Lipman and Michael Apple in the U.S.) is indispensable if we want to equip the next generation of educators and educational scholars with the tools for political engagement of public education, its dilemmas as well as possibilities. Feminist theory from Lather, Villenas, Luke and Gore, and Mirza expose the masculine structure of educational processes disguised as universals. Marxist scholars from Peter McLaren to Jean Anyon trace the material flows from the political economy to the division of intellectual labor in schools. Danny Solorzano, Roland Sintos Coloma, and Linda Tuhiwai Smith launch trenchant criticisms of racist-colonial vestiges in contemporary schooling within the racialized nation state. Finally, Youdell, Biesta, and Peters offer serious engagements of performative subject formation, the limits of humanism, and the knowledge economy, respectively. As powerful as these scholars and their insights are, the connective tissue that exists in this provisional list of scholars is not obvious. They seem to belong to the same hand but remain as separate as the fingers, to paraphrase Booker T. Washington (1986). On the surface, they comprise a loose set of adjacent commentaries on education. But their varieties, I would argue, do not eclipse their common purpose and family resemblance: to illuminate educational process through forms of criticism.

I am not simply arguing that educational scholars continue where Eisner left off in the 1970s. The kind of educational criticism that has since developed, and which I extend here through Said, brings with it a certain political edge to criticality. Questions of power and structure are central aspects of educational criticism that speaks not only to illumination (although it certainly supports that) but social emancipation. When Eisner's program gestures to the "structural," he gives a nod to Saussure's method rather than invoking the problem of immanent structures that place limitations on criticism by providing the horizon for the thinkable and therefore requires brutal self-reflection. In addition, early Critical Pedagogy up to the 1990s has always insisted that critical is precisely that mode of educational thought targeting structures that explain what kinds of human beings are possible in any given social formations. Finally, when Eisner mentions "critical theory," one senses its origin in aesthetic theory dating back to classical philosophy (see Adams, 1970), rather than the more recent Frankfurt School Critical Theory. Eisner would likely be more comfortable with Benjamin Bloom than Walter Benjamin. This is interesting in light of the radical cut that Horkheimer (1972) performs between what he called "traditional" vs. "critical theory," when he writes,

> The traditional idea of theory is based on scientific activity as carried on within the division of labor at a particular stage in the latter's development. It corresponds to the activity of the scholar which takes place alongside all the other activities of a society but in no immediately clear connection with them. In this view of theory, therefore, the real social function of science is not made manifest; it speaks not of what theory means in human life, but only of what it means in the isolated sphere in which for historical reasons it comes into existence. Yet as a matter of fact the life of society is the result of all the work done in the various sectors of production. . . . [Theorists] believe they are acting according to personal determinations, whereas in fact even in their most complicated calculations they but exemplify the working of an incalculable social mechanism. . . . A conception is needed which overcomes the onesidedness that necessarily arises when limited intellectual processes are detached from their matrix in the total activity of society.
>
> (pp. 197, 199)

Critical theory in Horkeimer's sense must deal with, although not only, the mode of production, more specifically capitalism, as a social structure that subverts both human thought and freedom. The Frankfurt School intellectuals from Horkheimer to Habermas provided a common language for critical pedagogues, whereby critique provides a way into educational problems that, even without administrative blueprints for solving them, poses their immanent structure as a limit to educational thought itself, making the study of language paramount – and here Eisner might agree. There are important departures from Eisner's program that this book hopefully develops by engaging Said, much of which Eisner's work did not touch upon but may be sympathetic with or perhaps foreshadowed.

Critique is the commitment to understanding contradictions in the human condition and our mutual implication in them, which is not conditioned by their resolution but an intellectual vocation in the ongoing project of liberation. It is less about throwing in the towel and more about entering the fray without the promise of guarantees or aiming for certainties. It regards history as structuring without determining our response to it. Educational thought centers criticism without necessarily valorizing the critic, opens phenomena in order to ask new questions rather than offer old answers, and leads to edification through continued dialogue about the educative functions of social life that is not reducible to schooling. Or as Said (2001) warns, "[C]riticism is radically misconceived if it tries to reify (a) the critic, (b) the text, (c) criticism" (*PPC*, p. 17). In other words, criticism should lead to more or further criticism, not less.

Contrapuntal Education and Criticism

In the remaining pages I have left, the new specialization centered on educational criticism I propose necessitates at least an outline. I do not want to err on the side of either an overly formed offering or an eschatological portrait of criticism. Although it would be too ambitious to outline Said's entire program of criticism here, it is worth identifying a couple strands of his thought as they implicate a general uptake of criticism for education. I would also stress that the preceding chapters on exile, knowledge, and the intellectual are part and parcel of Said's project of criticism and therefore are not separate from his ideas around contrapuntality. For instance, as Rizvi and Lingard (2006) observe,

> For him [Said] exile was not simply a state of deprivation, but also a privileged condition that enabled him to see multiple perspectives that needed to be reconciled in some principled fashion. In an homologous way he also saw the dangers and potential reinvigorations in theory which travelled both temporally and spatially. Following Adorno, Said also believed that the intellectual could, or at least should, never be at home in the world.
>
> (p. 302)

So contrapuntal criticism is based on taking the position of and seeing the social world from the optics of the exilic margins, where *nothing*, including the desire for home, is taken for granted. The intellectual acknowledges the fact and harms of coloniality alongside its hybridization of the colonial world where the colonizer and colonized, White and Black, center and periphery exist as complementarities and therefore rarely if ever occupy spaces of identity but rather of difference. But it is not hybridization as the intellectual version of body piercing because "contrapuntal criticism was devised as an alternative to hybridity, conjuring images more of independently directed harmonizations and contacts than of mixture and mutual complicity" (Brennan, 2005, p. 48). According to Brennan, this was Said's worry over the "oracular model of pedagogy" (p. 46) based on the sage expert, a cult figure at the head of the university seminar. Said's (2004) version of the hybrid is better captured as "amphibious" (*HDC*, p. 1).

Contrapuntal education proceeds by acknowledging power imposition from the top as well as a response to it from the bottom and therefore departs from determinisms that have dogged the educational left since at least Bowles and Gintis. Rizvi and Lingard (2006) describe, "By contrapuntal criticism Said suggested European culture needed to be read in relation to its spatial and political relations to empire, as well as in counterpoint to the works that colonized people themselves produced in response to colonial domination" (p. 301). This dual sensibility was also central to Adorno's (1973) understanding of the limitations of identitarianism, or positive identity, which is based on the repression of difference, requiring "negative dialectics" to excavate the hidden *differend* (Lyotard, 1992). And although Said's literary criticism is a different species from educational criticism, such that the latter contains aspects of practice that differ from the former, it is worthwhile to consider where Said's general insights into criticism are instructive for education. In particular, I would like now to focus on one aspect of his reconstruction of criticism through his use of *contrapuntality*.

At its best, criticism is about forging a world by participating in it as active subjects or agents of history in a sociality defined by coexistence and striving to live with difference. This intersubjective space requires a critic attuned to what Said calls "contrapuntality," or criticism that attests to historical experiences that crisscross each other at tangents, however obliquely (Mufti, 2005; Said, 2000, *Exile*). Taken from music, contrapuntal describes two independent melodies side by side in one song or score. Said takes this basic insight as a core principle of the politics or "fields of coexistence" (Said, 2004, *HDC*,

p. 141), from reading literary or philological works, to cultural dialogue, to the Israel-Palestine conflict. In other words, contrapuntal criticism is a form of resistance to practices of exclusion at both the literal and figurative levels, a way of reading experiences into one another as complementarities, inflected by but never independent of each other. Mufti (2005) recalls,

> Said's most influential contribution to these debates is of course the concept and metaphor – evocative, dense, and elusive at the same time – of contrapuntality, first employed in 1984 in the essay "Reflections on Exile," but finding its fullest elaboration in *Culture and Imperialism*.
>
> (p. 114)

As a form of reading and reception, contrapuntal analysis follows Péguy's "touching mode: criticism that openly seeks the assent and identification with it of its readers" (Said, 2000, *Exile*, p. 168). At once a musical term and a philosophical stance on social experience broadly speaking, contrapuntality is criticism with the other rather than about or for them. It takes music as its inspiration but Said transforms contrapuntality as a principle of criticism, indeed of social life.

There is something pedagogical in this orientation to the world, educational in what it has to teach us about the relationality of difference without falling prey to relativism. It promotes distinctness without domination, particularity without essentialism. For Said, the ultimate test case is the Palestinian condition throughout the world but certainly most felt in the occupied territories of the West Bank and Gaza. But contrapuntal analysis *goes all the way down* to academic culture and interrogates methods that incorporate the other through ethnographies that exoticize them, theories that sacrifice a concern with worldliness for textual autonomy, or a general lack of concern for human suffering. Said's break out study was Orientalism but his reach has extended past this important, albeit continuing, event. Contrapuntal analysis juxtaposes worlds previously considered incommensurate, a trait of truly modern life and cosmopolitan education.

First, an important part of contrapuntality is appreciating the role and centrality of language in the human condition, not as a textual practice but as evidence of real historical experience, often of suffering. For Said, "criticism is an act of love.... For an exile, criticism involves love for all the world, but it requires the clearest of description, analysis, and judgment of power's realities, especially its unjust imbalances" (Bové, 2005, p. 36). Victimhood is insufficient if it is not, at some point, intellectualized and universalized to include all sufferers, whereby the particularity of suffering must leave the body and enter universality of the human experience. This commitment to understanding suffering leads Said to reject what he calls "ultrapostmodern positions" that understand misery and liberation as texts or reducible to linguistic play (2004, *HDC*, p. 136). Said would likely not have kept the company of the vertiginous postmodernist, Jean Baudrillard (see Leonardo, 2003c). When Fanon (2008) begins *Black Skin, Whites Masks* with a chapter on "The Black Man and Language," it is not language qua language that Fanon has in mind but an injunction to force the European metropolis to think of its history together with colonized peripheries, like Algeria or Fanon's own Martinique, by understanding language within the colonial predicament. Similarly, Said appreciates language as *about something*, without being determined by that something. For Said, the colonial-imperial condition is not a linguistic problem that language may then resolve, even if we elevate the status of language.

Through language, educators understand that colonialism transacts and is constituted as a system of meaning, images, and allegories. This is not a mythical system in the sense that these significations are false or merely made up, as in the orthodox notion of ideology. Texts are not autonomous things in the world insofar as they conspire with social life, such as when history textbooks paint a distorted picture of Black families, particularly boys and men, as out of control and therefore needing to be controlled (Brown, 2011; Swartz, 1992). For instance, Anthony Brown (2011) surveyed the social science and education literature dating back to the 1930s to interrogate the "recycled discourses" and "*same old stories*" (p. 2052; italics in original) that use pathological or controlling images (see Collins, 2000) of Black families, particularly men. Employing Popkewitz's populational reasoning and Pride's conceptual narrative methodologies, Brown traces the consistent pattern of research that frames Blacks as deficient despite attempts by scholars, like E. Franklin Frazier and Du Bois, to shift the discourse. Often, these counternarratives existed alongside majoritarian narratives, such as the reframing of Black adaptive behavior alongside debilitating descriptions such as the Moynihan Report. Not unlike Said's discovery of Orientalist discourse across space and time, Brown uncovers the uncanny persistence of an almost unchanging portrayal of Black males in otherwise reputable and scientific research.

In this situation, Black bodies are not reducible to texts even if they are written into the history books that derogate them. The power of ideology makes these meanings *stick* because there is an existing and asymmetrical relation of power that binds the pathological depiction of blackness with the political economy of whiteness (see Thompson, 1984). Resistance to anti-black texts attempts to rip these interpellations from their basis. The opposite is whiteness' teflon resilience to textual attempts to dislodge it from the center.

An individual experiences suffering in its irreducible form, always unique to a single human organism. But human understanding, which is the task of criticism, registers the injury as an insult to the collective human group whose interconnections are defined minimally by a hermeneutics of empathy among strangers. Said (1983) describes,

> On the one hand, the individual mind registers and is very much aware of the collective whole, context, or situation in which it finds itself. On the other hand, precisely because of this awareness – a worldly self-situating, a sensitive response to the dominant culture – that the individual consciousness is not naturally and easily a mere child of the culture, but a historical actor in it. And because of that perspective, which introduces circumstance and distinction where there had only been conformity and belonging, there is distance, or what we might also call *criticism*.
>
> (*WTC*, p. 15; my italics)

The task of criticism is not sentimental empathy with others by abandoning concern for one's own suffering. This lacks self-awareness. But criticism is also not provincial by isolating one's injury, unable to recognize others' suffering on their own terms because they are different from one's own. This lacks historical awareness. Educational criticism cultivates the ability to be in touch with our human flesh and then detach from it in order to appropriate the other as we would allow them to appropriate us. This is the task of criticism, the vacillation between self-recognition and self-estrangement (not in the Marxist sense of alienation) for the purposes of being in touch and an openness to being touched.

For Said, language is central to criticism, at once representing language's excess and poverty. Without language in all its variegated expressions, there is no criticism. But as an apparatus of representation, language is often more or less than actual experience: the first a romanticizing impulse of experience, the second limiting our understanding of it through the limited language we have at our disposal to name experience in the first place. A contrapuntal language practice acknowledges language's excess and poverty while claiming

> that the intellectual's provisional home is the domain of an exigent, resistant, intransigent art into which, alas, one can neither retreat nor search for solutions. But only in that precarious exilic realm can one first truly grasp the difficulty of what cannot be grasped and then go forth to try anyway.
>
> (Said, 2004, *HDC*, p. 144)

In a Sysiphean manner, contrapuntal educators push words up the hill as an attempt to capture linguistically a more complete picture of historical experience only to have words roll back down to remind us of the inadequate understanding necessitated by the language currently available to us. But in doing so, we redouble and recommit to the project of historical understanding. It is this spirit of human striving and restlessness whereby contrapuntal hermeneutics is borne out of struggle.

Not unlike Freire's description, Said's version of the contrapuntal exile appears as one who is never satisfied, placid, or secure, one who moves to a different calendar, outside of habitual order, a fickle and decentered nomad. Or as Bhabha notes,

> It is from the turbulence of wars, occupations, segregations, and evictions that there emerges a resistant hope that these unsettled energies of place and displacement will settle into a design for living with shared borders and contrapuntal histories. . . . Polyphony and contrapuntality are amongst Said's most commonly used poetic and political metaphors to describe the procedures of philological reception and resistance.
>
> (2005, pp. 14–15)

In the traffic of human culture and history, we are guided more by the multiculturalism of James Banks rather than Citibank's, certainly not NATO's "military humanism" when it bombed Yugoslavia in 1999 (Said, 2004, *HDC*, p. 7). A contrapuntal reading of social life is ultimately a teacher of the possibility in language that surrenders neither to surplus hopefulness nor hopelessness. This is why the linguistic animal differs from the non-linguistic one, through the fact that the former is condemned to the state of hoping as part of personal or collective agency. In comparison, a snail is cute but its day-to-day existence is no symbol of hope.

Second, through contrapuntality, a more connected world history emerges, what Said was fond of calling "worldliness." We begin to comprehend the reality that it is difficult or impossible to assess France or Britain's greatness (or the U.S.'s for that matter) without accounting for their role in colonial accumulation or participating in the riches (more accurately robbery) of enslavement and other crimes against humanity. This peculiar feeling allows subjects to traverse the bridges over the Seine or Thames Rivers to marvel at French civilization and English modernity while remarking on the signs of colonialism on the same walkways that stain this otherwise awe-inspiring promenade. Contrapuntal awareness allows us to hold both positions about the pleasure and displeasure of human progress, what Walter Benjamin once described as civilization's barbaric side (as cited by Said, 2004, *HDC*, p. 23) or reason's ability to usher in the Enlightenment only then to colonize Africa and other non-Europeans or deride women as irrational, all in the name of reason (Horkheimer & Adorno, 1976). Similarly, in education, suburban schools' achievement must be considered side by side with divestment in urban and ghetto schools (Anyon, 1997). Or, more specifically, White and Asian success is often at the cost of failure to educate or commit to Black and Latinx children's uplift. This is less a finger-pointing exercise, even less a strategy to instill guilt in advantaged communities or argue for their demise. It is to admit that there is often the case of "two Americas" at play here in what philosopher Charles Mills (1997), borrowing from sociologist Pierre van den Berghe, would call a *herrenvolk* educational system, one black, the other white. Contrapuntal, educational criticism is not just woke but sees life with both eyes open.

The turn to language and discourse in educational theory has been felt at least as early as 1980s, intensely during the 1990s, and in a crisis by the 2000s. Giroux's influential writings from *Theory and Resistance in Education* (1983) onwards, to Patti Lather's (1991) deconstructive feminism in *Getting Smart*, to Biesta's travails from Foucault, to Derrida and Ranciere, point education to the centrality of language within criticism. Not evident during the 1970s despite Eisner's urging, the growth of criticism in education, particularly what Giroux (1988) calls a "language of criticism and possibility" from the 1980s on, was made possible by the turn away from a certain vulgar materialism. In its place was a committed and serious consideration of the subjectification function of language as a discursive system that constitutes and then positions normed "humans" in what it means to construct the education, as opposed to the socialization, function of schooling (Biesta, 2010). Foundational understandings that were *de rigueur* as a result of the hegemony of humanism and science, among other metanarratives, become suspect as Bowles and Gintis slowly become eclipsed by the likes of Judith Butler and David T. Goldberg (see Gottesman, 2016). What this development unearths is the appreciation that the human was invented by humanism, Euro-humanism specifically. It goes without saying that all people are homo sapiens but only some are human; or as Charles Mills (1997) describes the cut, some are human while others are humanoids. By the 2000s, the excesses of the turn to language became a source of discontent for some educational theorists, as McLaren and Scatamburlo-D'Annibale (2005) complain that whereas Marx improved upon Hegel by moving away from fighting phrases with phrases, poststructuralism opposes signification with signification. Not a hell of a lot of difference to card-carrying Marxists.

This tension regarding language notwithstanding, the effect of recent theorizing and criticism since Foucault cannot be reduced to a fad. For his own part, Said finds a problem in Foucault's (1991) insistence on the disappearance of the author, preferring instead on being cognizant of our own traces left in the grooves of our writing or speech. That said, Said's *Orientalism* contains a good dose of Foucauldian inspiration. Said's nod to Gramsci's (1971) notion of creating an inventory from the infinity of traces history has left in us is palpable as well. Not really one to mince his words, Said has this to say about the idea that texts do not connect with actuality:

> This is a view I do not agree with, not simply because texts in fact are in the world but also because as texts they place themselves – and

> indeed are themselves, by soliciting the world's attention. Moreover, their manner of doing this is to place restraints upon what can be done with them interpretively.
>
> (Said, 1983, *WTC*, p. 40)

A firm believer in texts and their contexts, Said insists on the powerful relationship between language and the social world. There are "too many . . . circumstances [that] implicate the text in actuality, even if a text may also be considered a silent printed object with its own unheard *melodies*" (Said, 1983, *WTC*, pp. 49–50; my italics). He shares an affinity with Volosinov who links ideology and material existence when the Russian critic writes, "The understanding of any sign, whether inner or outer, occurs inextricably tied in with the *situation in which the sign is implemented*" (Volosinov, 2006, p. 37; italics in original). Although Volosinov begins from the perspective of class struggle when he interprets the system of signs – that is, concepts (or their imprint through words) and meaning – the link between language and its social situation allows Said to affirm a worldly attitude towards the notion of text. If this inheres a family resemblance with Freire and Macedo's (1987) dialectical literacy program when they encourage a reading of the word and the world, Said's educational relevance is established.

Contrapuntal is Said's assertion of an earth-connected analysis. I do not want to overinterpret this opening as somehow in line with what we know about indigenous analysis of education as a concern with pedagogies of land and territory within a decolonization project (Tuck & Yang, 2012). Said's project is more akin to an "earthly world" analysis, a praxis of worldliness that places literature within the ligature of the social body (Roman, 2006, p. 395; see also Singh & Greenlaw, 1998). Or as Said states,

> My position is that texts are worldly, to some degree they are events, and even when they appear to deny it, they are nevertheless a part of the social world, human life, and of course the historical moments in which they are located and interpreted.
>
> (Said, 1983, *WTC*, p. 4)

A scholar of letters, Said was committed to a hermeneutics of the text but his requirements suggest that even before students are encouraged to make sense of their experience, recruit science to objectify and explain it, educators recognize the importance of witnessing their students' concrete historical experience, of how their bodies register it. This does not mean that the experience speaks for itself, which therefore requires theory to illuminate it and Said considered it trite to reject theory as trivial. Before illuminating our experience, theory must speak *through* the subject and not just *about* them, even if the subject occasionally misunderstands their experience.

As feminists from Hartsock (1987) to Harding (1991) have distinguished, and Marx before them (see Smith, 1989), standpoint epistemology does not suggest that the speaking subject, in this case Said's exegete, is correct by virtue of having had the experience of being wronged. Although Marx's original notion of "false consciousness" is now out of favor as excessively cognitivist and objectivist, it pointed to the possibility of the subject's misrecognition of their own condition or interest. Since Althusser (1971) and on, an affective, rather than cognitive or epistemological, theory of ideology puts educators in a better position to appreciate and assess students' investment in their own pre-critical meanings, which must be reckoned with and not be circumvented in the name of criticality. This is Paul Willis' (1977) gambit in *Learning to Labor* as he documents the lads' partial glimpse into their own domination to which they submit as they disqualify themselves from the race for credentials by "laffing" off school culture (see McGrew for a review of Willis' influence, 2011). In the end, the lads fulfill the reproductive functions of school but Willis is clear that the process of hegemony includes their consent, not as dupes but also not as completely self-transparent subjects. This move is nuanced because Willis distances himself from reproductive theorists, such as the micro-sociology of Bernstein (1977a, 1977b) to the macro-sociology of Bourdieu (1977) and Bourdieu and Passeron (1990), and Bowles and Gintis (1976), without denying that reproduction occurs (Willis, 1981). After all, the official subtitle of Willis' book is *How Working Class Kids Get Working Class Jobs*.

As another concrete example, the particularity of racial experience is where meanings may derive their force for some students on whom race literally leaves its mark on the body as part of the racial habitus. But to Said, the concreteness of this immediacy has to leave the racialized body, as it were, and become abstracted because meaning has to be objectified through a language and system of meaning that are both public and social. It is as if experience at the bodily level is too concrete, too private, and must become public in order to find its larger significance, its broader human connections. Said joins the reconstruction of "experience" as the sole basis for understanding since experience never speaks for itself but through a discursive relationship that reminds educators of the interplay among institutions, culture, and meaning. The body may never forget the experience but it requires the work of language to remember it. At this point, the universal themes of oppression arise and different groups are able to dialogue about the general experience of racial forms of suffering that, while experienced specifically, are not in the end incommensurable (see Flecha, 1999; cf. Tuck & Yang, 2012). Infantilization, derogation, alienation from others, self-hatred, unmet needs, misrecognition, and social constraints are only some of the universal signs of life in the margins. But so are resistance, resilience, and refusal. The dialectics of experience with oppression are not without its dangers as essentialist self-concepts threaten to imitate the problems we aim to transcend. Self-pity, righteousness, and conspicuous authenticity result from unchecked essentialism.

Third, contrapuntal criticism is a secular move against religious criticism. To reiterate, for Said religiosity is not a reference to organized religion but a general descriptor for an ideology that treats certain forms of knowledge as sacred or to be discovered rather than created by humans in Vico's sense. This should be familiar to any educator who paid an ounce of attention to the cultural wars of the 1990s, a time of intense debates regarding the curriculum to which I referred in Chapter 1. From Allan Bloom's *The Closing of the American Mind* to Saul Bellow's incendiary, and, to some, racist, comments about the absence of an "African Proust," multicultural reform from history (see Symcox, 2002) to social studies (Banks, 1993) swept across the educational system from kindergarten to postdoctoral studies. Bellow, Bloom, Babbit, Bush I and II, and former Secretary of Education Bennett are a dream team with whom Said would not likely play. Bemoaning the professionalization of the critic, Said (1983) writes, "Once an intellectual, the modern critic has become a cleric in the worst sense of the word" (*WTC*, p. 292). Against the notion that Eurocentric knowledge is "culture"-free and then elevated to human "Culture" by followers of Matthew Arnold (1867), the deepest multicultural reform of the canon is consistent with Said's reformulation of knowledge as human-made rather than divine.

The turn to secularity within educational criticism affirms the project of contrapuntal multiculturalism that knowledge is a human creation and therefore open to the greatness as well as fallibility of that species. No originary point of emanation, no center without its complementary margin, no ordering of human history without some sense of violence in the act of ordering, no divine originality that does not already assume the human hand, the absence of religion and the presence of actuality – this is secular interpretation in a nutshell. Following Said, Mitchell pronounces that "*sacred knowledge* is a kind of oxymoron" (2005, p. 102; italics in original), by which he suggests that what humans have done can be undone, if only to begin again in order to be different from oneself. Said takes irreverence literally as the absence of worship for knowledge, for authority, and for the expert. At the same time, he embodies a contradictory conservatism in his respect for his adversaries when he writes,

> I take criticism so seriously as to believe that, even in the very midst of a battle in which one is unmistakably on one side against another, there should be criticism, because there must be critical consciousness if there are to be issues, problems, values, even lives to be fought for.
>
> (Said, 1983, *WTC*, p. 28)

Authentic criticism requires self-critique.

In place of religiosity (or its nation-state cousin, patriotism), we have beginnings, dialogue, and responsibility. Apropos to Du Bois' (1989) pronouncement about the problem of the color line at the beginning of the twentieth century, "the religious line would be the problem of the late twentieth century" (Brennan, 2005, p. 47). Schools, particularly public schools, have fought the good fight regarding the merits of a radical reconstruction of the curriculum. As a form of symbolic violence (Bourdieu & Passeron, 1990), the curriculum's power is most efficiently hidden when it parades as predetermined, as apparently having no origins in human culture even if your garden-variety educator understands that Eurocentrism comes from a place and time. Despite multiculturalization of the school curriculum for several decades since the 1980s, it is difficult to dislodge the tradition that treats worthwhile knowledge, at least its modern form, as originating from Europe. Therefore, studying Shaka Zulu will be a cheap imitation of the study of Shakespeare. This is partly what Said calls religious knowledge, not unlike the colonial difference between the French patois spoken by the Algerian or Black Antillean when compared to speaking French by the French (Bourdieu, 1991; Fanon, 2008). Origins are vertical by default, whereas beginnings are horizontal.

Said's preference for "beginnings" departs from the epistemology of origins. Because beginning is a choice, it is a multiplicity by necessity as there are many beginnings, whereas there is usually only one origin. There is no such thing as *the* beginning. But there is ever only beginning at a time and place, which maintains its specificity as having begun from a certain location and moment, which cannot be repeated by another beginning. Once the beginning has commenced, the beginner cannot repeat it, much the same way that a flowing river's water has already moved on. Because of this contingency, the agent of beginnings is not stuck in either a reified history or an unalterable situation. It is contrapuntal because "intention is the link between idiosyncratic view and the communal concern" (Said, 1985, *Beginnings*, p. 13) and the beginner is never alone. Neither is beginning an exercise in teleology because it does not speed towards a chosen end but may wind up in just as many possible destinations as beginnings. Because it is more or less freely chosen, beginning is active whereas origin is passive, the former leading to more choices to be made as a result of having committed to previous ones. It is possible to imagine that due to the sheer repetition of choosing to begin similarly, authors invent an origin, such as what Said finds in the pervasiveness of Orientalist texts that seem to speak to each other without intention, as if conspiring. Following Said, Bilgrami (2005) notes that "beginnings are constrained by the *intention* of the agent who writes and imagines; and intentions bring with them a *method*, a method of inquiry ... one cannot *intend* to be original" (pp. 27, 28; italics in original). Originary concerns betray a certain fetish with lineage insofar as iterations of or variations in ideas ultimately return to their primordial source, tributaries of the original fount: usually Europe.

This impasse is not unlike the excessive determinism that Marxism has been accused of regarding the base-superstructure metaphor that slingshots culture, language, and other superstructural features back to their economic basis. To Raymond Williams (1977), criticism is crippled by a chauvinism that judges the effectivity of culture by the tape of an economic rationale. It was Williams – with Stuart Hall, Paul Willis, and other Brits – who took it upon himself to rework Marxism's relationship with the potential power of culture, folk or otherwise. In education and around the same period of writing in the mid-1970s, the critique of root causes cast a shadow over an otherwise complete and thorough Marxist analysis of schooling found in Bowles and Gintis' (1976) *Schooling in Capitalist America*. I do not need to rehearse here either the main points or deep influence of *Schooling* in educational criticism (see Gottesman, 2016). Said inaugurates a new metaphor in the term "beginnings," which chips away at the excesses of originary thinking. Said joins the company of Deleuze and Guattari's (1983) theory of the "rhizome" while maintaining his distance from ultrapostmodern theory whose influence was beginning to circulate in the humanities and thereafter the social sciences, including education.

The turn (or return?) to beginnings is useful for educational criticism. Beginnings suggest a basic methodological question: How do we proceed? In effect, we must choose a beginning, whether temporal or spatial, usually both. No story, for example, begins from an origin, but from a choice an author makes *in medias res*, a project already underway. It only confirms that something has in fact commenced, and by commencing, constrains the possible interpretations of a given text or author. Said is not naïve because he acknowledges that beginnings are not equal and some beginnings are authorized as such, by institutions, by positionality, and by power. But it is a democratizing impulse to suggest that anyone can indeed begin and assert their intention, which is the human trace that allows Said to refuse Foucault's (1991) provocation in pronouncing the death of the author. From this beginning, the ends are not predictable and the destination is undetermined by virtue of the beginning, traveling without guarantees. Yet we start, as start we must.

There are limits, of course, or those beginnings we did not choose, such as *filiation*, like birth, nationality, and, in most circumstances, family. But as Said (1983) reminds us, we choose our *affiliation* such as conviction, circumstance, effort, and deliberation (*WTC*, pp. 16 and 20). From these correlates, we begin and therefore proceed without a clear blueprint other than committing to our choices or changing our interpretations when appropriate or convinced by another's commitments. This perspective smacks of existentialism insofar as we are condemned to choose a beginning. It is in this sense that beginnings contain in them a sense of the human rather than the divine. It is less the idea that Eve originated from Adam's rib and more the image of both of them walking out of paradise, hand in hand. From beginnings, a future awaits rather than a past that haunts, which is forward rather than backward looking. Yet it is not a radical indeterminacy that Said argues for, but a contingency informed by the concrete conditions found in a particular struggle. It shares sympathies with Freire's (1993) commitment to a future always in the making, an openness to a politics of incompleteness whose uncertainty is mitigated by a sense of radical responsibility for a world that we make. A reflective and responsible author is precisely the kind that prevents the wrong kind of interpretation of their work, or at least makes it difficult to co-opt for exactly the opposite, intended ends. This is the critical spirit.

Linda Tuhiwai Smith's (1999) now classic text, *Decolonizing Methodologies*, goes a long way to explain what is at stake with respect to the colonial-imperial history of educational research. Known as a founding scholar of indigenous education worldwide, Smith indicts western-driven methodologies that fixate on and attempts to fix non-westerners. In Fanon's (2008) sense of "Look, a Negro!", this objectifying gaze or fixation turns native subjects into *native objects* for western consumption through knowledge production, not unlike Said's contention that Orientalism was fundamentally a knowledge relation between the knower (i.e., Europeans) and known (i.e., Orientals). It transfixes both the Occident and Orient, reducing their character and caricaturing their culture. To call this a critique of deficit perspectives underestimates the damage that western-centric protocols have unleashed on Maori and other indigenous peoples when instrumental reason reduces their knowledge as lacking value because it is inapprehensible through scientific precepts. Derogated as myths – not in the sense of narratives that bind the social but plainly false – indigenous epistemology becomes a foil that allows European epistemology – the true and beautiful – to assert itself at once as an ideological and a material force. Worse, knowledge production through Eurocentric epistemology becomes a way to control the indigenous lifeworld because it sanctions interventions that save indigenous people from themselves. Contrapuntal educational research is not the assertion of indigenous rightness, plain and simple, as a counter to cultural imperialism. It is a mirror to hold up to European humanism's inhumanity towards those it reduces to nonhumans, to force westerners to ask not only what they have done to the Other but to reflect on what they have become in the process.

Fourth, contrapuntal educational criticism works against dogma and totalizing perspectives. It is related to Said's rejection of religious criticism in favor of secular thought. It is no small irony that despite being a public critic of humanism for much of his long and distinguished career, Said publishes a defense of humanism in 2004. In *Humanism and Democratic Criticism*, Said asserts a bold claim to criticize humanism in the name of humanism, arguing for a non-humanist humanism, which he says points to a "conflict between my avowed and unmistakable humanistic bias and the antihumanism of my subject and my approach toward it" (Said, 2004, *HDC*, p. 8). Biesta (2010) seems to agree when he calls attention to humanism's inhumanity, by which he means that humanism reduces incalculable and multiple humans under an inhumane rubric, such as the reduction of humans under the sign of reason from Kant onwards. Said's uptake of humanism is consistent with his intellectual resourcefulness to avoid rejecting *in toto* a perspective like humanism, against which he has been at loggerheads for most of his career.

It is not humanism qua humanism to which Said objects but self-proclaimed humanists' abuses of other humans under the aegis of a self-congratulating humanism, a dehumanizing humanism. If Said gestures to post-humanism, it is not the "after" of humanism that he signals with the prefix but as with much of post-theorizing, the "post" indicates a fundamental ambivalence with the -ism that follows it. The move is less against humanism as such but an interrogation of its premises in order to revise its assumptions of who, conceptually speaking, belongs to the category of the "human." To the extent that anti- or post-humanism lurks in Said's last works, its goal is to repair humanism's harms perpetrated on the cursed share of that extolled family. Said's gambit does not prevent intellectuals from generating new interpellations to replace the human, but even such attempts must deal with the systematic exclusion of certain populations from humanity currently happening at the planetary level. Therefore, finding ways to expand the membership of the human to be more inclusive of people heretofore kept out of that club becomes a necessary step that cannot be leapfrogged. Said's unwillingness to abdicate humanism to its pretenders suggests this search for a more humanizing humanism.

Said's rejection of dogma did not prevent him from sounding dogmatic on occasion. His self-characterization appears this way:

> Were I to use one word consistently along with *criticism* (not as a modification but as an emphatic) it would be *oppositional*. . . . In its suspicion of totalizing concepts, in its discontent with reified objects, in its impatience with guilds, special interests, imperialized fiefdoms, and orthodox habits of mind, criticism is most itself and, if the paradox can be tolerated, most unlike itself at the moment it starts turning into organized dogma.
>
> (Said, 1983, *WTC*, p. 29; italics in original)

Theoretical closure is anathema to the critical spirit and criticism suffers from dogma. Steeped in European letters, Said was also one of its fiercest critics; a leftist incendiary in his commentaries, he was a self-described conservative in certain tastes, music being one of them; a supporter of Palestinian independence until his death, Said would have nothing to do with the project of identity politics.

Interpreting European literature in contrapuntal juxtaposition to non-western writing, Said's urging is to challenge, reread and re-examine, not distort or reject, western culture, which may lead to the opposite of Orientalism, or Occidentalism. However, Said's provocation does not imply that the two are symmetrical such that Occidentalism is a secondary problem to Orientalism, but a problem nevertheless. Decisive in his prose, Said was nevertheless fond of bafflement, the incongruous, the irreconcilable, the untidy (Mitchell, 2005). Said was eccentric only to the casual reader, but ex-centric to people who truly appreciated him. In other words, Said spoke from the margins, outside of center. Educational criticism informed by Said's opening is not paradigmatic in Thomas Kuhn's (1970) sense of that word. This means there is no gospel theory that can save education from its discontents. But a politics of criticism with no guarantees, as Stuart Hall (1996) once asserted, is sensitive to the changing needs of developing or future generations, and not in the sentimental sense that schools exist "for the kids" at the same time that they forsake children.

Finale: Criticism as an Act of Freedom

Criticism is a committed act of freedom while paying attention to its investments that otherwise subvert it. Said's is a protean hermeneutics and he was

> the scientist of antinomies. He approached the physics of culture in terms of a quantum paradigm, one that it is neither straightforward nor backward, but some combination of both, that things are never entirely black and white, but sometimes white can be black, and sometimes both.
>
> (Symes, 2006, p. 312)

Educational critics looking for a linear explanation of constraint and marginalization, and their opposite, freedom and emancipation, will be disappointed in Said's framework. He does not provide easy answers, but those who work in the interstices or educational borderlands (see Villenas, 2010) will find a narrow beam in Said's ideas that, when balance suits, provides sufficient footing.

Education scholars should find purchase in Said's complexity in light of the seemingly intractable problem of educational disparities that resists silver bullet analyses. One move in the chess game of schooling necessitates a corresponding shift in its overall structure so that tinkering with inequality has shown over and again an undeniable limitation. An aggregate or composite look at said inequalities approaches education's complexity that escapes singular axis explanations, like race, class, or gender (Leonardo & Grubb, 2019). But this fact does not vitiate against *beginning* with race, class, or gender as a particular focus that resonates within specific conjunctures, which does not suggest that it *ends* there. In an intellectual climate where Crenshaw's (1991) concept of "intersectionality" has "gone viral" (Bartlett, 2017), it is not uncommon that any analysis that begins with a social axis is met with disapproving eyes at least or hostility at worst, in the name of intersectionality (for a review, see Harris & Leonardo, 2018). But the preference to analyze everything in one fell swoop, almost always a failed project of criticism, may derail an otherwise powerful focus on race, class, or gender because it does not leap off the page as a "theory of everything." Intersectionality was an innovation to explain more, but the impatience with race, class, or gender analysis that does not co-implicate them may end up explaining less, as in prose that strings "the economic, cultural, political, and social" to little or no effect. Explaining social oppression *in toto* can appear as totalitarian, in fact sometimes debilitating or paralyzing, and the misuses or abuses of intersectional analysis is a sign of its commodification and domestication. An essay criticizing Crenshaw as insufficiently intersectional may be just around the corner.

Sensibility for the contrapuntal in educational criticism means that interdependency is more the case than the exception. For example, in the U.S. White and Black lives are intertwined, whose destinies are inextricably historical and shot through with one another. As such, white advantage is often evidence of black disadvantage, white wealth as parasitic of black wealth (Oliver & Shapiro, 1997). Criticism in education is currently ad hoc and haphazardly organized. Under the aegis of educational criticism, it is possible to reimagine critics as a community of intellectuals. To build a movement around educational criticism, we might heed Coser's advice,

> First, intellectuals need an audience, a circle of people to whom they can address themselves and who can bestow recognition. Such an audience will also, as a rule, provide economic rewards, but the prestige or esteem accorded to the intellectual by his public, his psychic income, may often be more important to him than his economic return. Second, intellectuals require regular contact with their fellow intellectuals, for only through such communication can they evolve common standards of method and excellence, common norms to guide their conduct. Despite popular myth to the contrary, most intellectuals cannot produce their work in solitude, but need the give and take of debate and discussion with their peers in order to develop their ideas. Not all intellectuals are gregarious, but most of them need to test their own ideas in exchange with those they deem their equals.
>
> (as cited by Said, 1983, *WTC*, pp. 79–80)

Of course, there are the usual pitfalls worth keeping in mind such as the contradictions of institutionalizing educational criticism, the gender and racial politics of participation as well as recognition, and careerism. That said, forging ahead with educational criticism is a politics of engagement, which is an act that promotes education rather than the educated.

Said's offering of the contrapuntal uses the music of hermeneutics and the hermeneutics of music to showcase the beauty of human interpretation when it shows deep concern and commitment for the other. Said was primarily known as a comparatist, "But for me, he was always, really, a musician, in the deepest sense of the term" (Barenboim, 2005, p. 166), whose "aesthetic polestars were music and literature" (Mitchell, 2005, p. 104). Educational criticism is thus like listening to music, at once enjoying the lyrics or the score while not losing sight of the melodies that shift and turn to signal transitions. Educational critics simultaneously register the displeasure of modern disparities in school resources, attrition rates and rates of expulsion, and general neglect of entire swathes of the population, with the pleasure that comes with a critical analysis of them. Pleasure and displeasure are constitutive of criticism that is contrapuntal. In the end, authentic criticism in education is as a fugue, maintaining an openness that other composers, in this case educators, appropriate and continue in their own song, reaching a crescendo in what Walt Whitman once called a "native grand opera" (see Cmiel, 1994), or in a more contemplative mood, what Wordsworth called the "still sad music of humanity" (Said, 1983, *WTC*, p. 74). Said's work is surely only one instrument among many, but surely the song is richer with him in it. Contrapuntal is a metaphor but not only in the sense of a clever trope to illuminate social dynamics, rather one that aims to eliminate human suffering.

As we enter the third decade of the third millennium, crises in civil society spread like wildfire across nations like the U.S., Great Britain, Australia, France, Germany, parts of Scandinavia, and other liberal democracies. Populist movements articulate with interests among diverse politics from neo-fascism to neoliberalism and neocolonialism. Said would have been disheartened to see such a development and the instability it has caused, despite that his work foreshadowed or could have predicted such wholesale violence. His appeal for respect for difference as the prerequisite to what he simply called coexistence needs reiterating now more than ever. Populist fundamentalism is at once a cry against the inertia of liberal governments and fissures in global capital as well as, unfortunately, a battle cry misplaced against already targeted groups through discourses of denigration: of immigrants, of Blacks, of women, and of Muslims. Eerily on point, Said writes,

> What this transformation means is nothing less than that nativist cultural traditions that pretend to authenticity and aboriginal priority can now be recognized as the great patently false and misleading fundamentalist ideology of our time. Those still clinging to it are the falsifiers and reductivists, the fundamentalists and deniers, whose doctrines must be criticized for what they have left out, denigrate, demonize, and dehumanize on presumably humanistic grounds.
>
> (Said, 2004, *HDC*, p. 48)

Trump's trumpeting of a false era attempts to reinstall White men's unearned privileges and Putin wants to put Russia in its previous seat at the global power table. Educators are reminded of the incivility of civil society when contrapuntal sensibilities are exchanged for contrarian politics.

Said's lifework has much purchase for explaining the failings of our time. But its power and relevance are not limited to naming only the negativity that divides a people. For Said, criticism, like educational criticism, contains a utopic thrust. It is guided by denunciation as an intellectual form that annunciates a better and possible world precisely by criticizing the world, not as a text but an actual one. When, for example, national borders are weaponized as if they were the property of the few or a group of self-appointed nativists, an alternative and more complex picture of humanism resists the temptation to join nativism's logic of a descent into permanent war. Seen through Said's eyes, educational criticism turns the social world into a classroom, a seminar where experimenting with ideas goes hand in hand with experimenting with forms of coexistence.

I wrote this book in the context of a social world that appears more like a cacophony of grinding or harsh sounds than a concert. It is disconcerting. In the national context where I write and work, the U.S. is mired in divisions many others and I have not witnessed for many decades, despite the awareness that something like this has happened before (e.g., the Vietnam War era, Nixon's presidency, or the like). It would be easy to blame President Trump for leading U.S. citizens into this quagmire, but he has a chorus that follows him even if he orchestrates them. Education, in the sense that differs from the institution of schooling, suffers from this condition and its edifying function gives way to its stultifying function. It is getting more and more difficult to hear the notes as extremism and emotionalism prefer to shout and shut down opposing views. We do not yet fully comprehend the damage that the younger generation is incurring and talks of a "deep divide" are only the tip of the iceberg or the fin of the shark that swims beneath. An educated criticism is needed more than ever, which is a joint vocation that makes more or further criticism possible, rather than shutting it down. The exile, rather than the expert, becomes our north star, and the analysis of earth's soil our positive obsession.

REFERENCES

Adams, H. (Ed.). (1970). *Critical theory since Plato*. New York: Harcourt Brace Jovanovich, Publishers.
Adorno, T. (1973). *Negative dialectics* (E. B. Ashton, Trans.). New York: Continuum.
Adorno, T. (1991). *The culture industry* (J. Bernstein, Ed.). New York: Routledge.
Alcoff, L. M. (2015). *The future of whiteness*. Malden, MA: Polity Press.
Althusser, L. (1971). *Lenin and philosophy* (B. Brewster, Trans.). New York: Monthly Review Press.
Althusser, L. (1976). *Essays in self-criticism* (G. Lock, Trans.). London: Humanities Press.
Anyon, J. (1997). *Ghetto schooling: A political economy of urban educational reform*. New York: Teachers College Press.
Appiah, K. (1990). Racisms. In D. Goldberg (Ed.), *Anatomy of racism* (pp. 3–17). Minneapolis: University of Minnesota Press.
Apple, M. (2000). *Official knowledge: Democratic education in a conservative age* (2nd ed.). New York: Routledge and Kegan Paul. First published in 1979.
Apple, M. (2019). *Ideology and curriculum* (4th ed.). New York: Routledge. First published in 1979.
Arnold, M. (1867). *Culture and anarchy*. New Haven: Yale University Press.
Aronowitz, S., & Giroux, H. (1985). *Education under siege*. South Hadley, MA: Bergin & Garvey.
Au, W. (2007). Vygotsky and Lenin on learning: The parallel structures of individual and social development. *Science & Society*, *71*(3), 273–298.
Auerbach, E. (1953). *Mimesis: The representation of reality in western literature*. Princeton: Princeton University Press.

REFERENCES

Bachelard, G. (1964). *The poetics of space* (M. Jolas, Trans.). New York: Orion Press.

Backer, D. (2018). Interpellation, counterinterpellation, and education. *Critical Education*, 9(12), 1–21. Retrieved from http://ojs.library.ubc.ca/index.php/criticaled/article/view/186408

Banks, J. (1993). Multicultural literacy and curriculum reform. In J. Noll (Ed.), *Taking sides* (7th ed., pp. 219–226). Guilford: The Dushkin Publishing Group.

Banks, J. (2006). *Race, culture, and education*. New York: Routledge.

Barenboim, D. (2005). Maestro. In H. Bhabha & W. J. T. Mitchell (Eds.), *Edward Said: Continuing the conversation* (pp. 163–167). Chicago: The University of Chicago Press.

Bartlett, T. (2017, May 21). When a theory goes viral. *Chronicle of Higher Education*. Retrieved June 30, 2017, from www.chronicle.com/article/The-Intersectionality-Wars/240095

Baudrillard, J. (1994). *Simulacra and simulations*. Ann Arbor: University of Michigan Press.

Bernstein, B. (1977a). Social class, language and socialization. In J. Karabel & A. H. Halsey (Eds.), *Power and ideology in education* (pp. 473–486). Oxford: Oxford University Press.

Bernstein, B. (1977b). Class pedagogies: Visible and invisible. In J. Karabel & A. H. Halsey (Eds.), *Power and ideology in education* (pp. 511–534). Oxford: Oxford University Press.

Bhabha, H. (2005). Adagio. In H. Bhabha & W. J. T. Mitchell (Eds.), *Edward Said: Continuing the conversation* (pp. 7–16). Chicago: The University of Chicago Press.

Biesta, G. (2001). "Preparing for the incalculable": Deconstruction, justice and the question of education. In G. J. J. Biesta & D. Egea-Kuehne (Eds.), *Derrida & education* (pp. 32–54). New York: Routledge.

Biesta, G. (2010). Education after the death of the subject: Levinas and the pedagogy of interruption. In Z. Leonardo (Ed.), *Handbook of cultural politics and education* (pp. 289–300). Rotterdam, The Netherlands: Sense Publishers.

Bilgrami, A. (2005). Interpreting a distinction. In H. Bhabha & W. J. T. Mitchell (Eds.), *Edward Said: Continuing the conversation* (pp. 26–35). Chicago: The University of Chicago Press.

Bloom, A. (1987). *The closing of the American mind*. New York: Simon & Schuster Inc.

Bobbitt, J. F. (1918). *The curriculum*. New York: Houghton Mifflin Co.

Bonilla-Silva, E. (2001). *White supremacy and racism in the post-civil rights era*. Boulder: Lynne Rienner Publishers.

Bonilla-Silva, E. (2003). *Racism without racists: Color-blind racism and the persistence of racial inequality in the United States*. Lanham, MD: Rowman & Littlefield.

Bonilla-Silva, E., Goar, C., & Embrick, D. (2006). When Whites flock together: The social psychology of White habitus. *Critical Sociology*, *32*(2–3), 229–253.

Bourdieu, P. (1977). Cultural reproduction and social reproduction. In J. Karabel & A. H. Halsey (Eds.), *Power and ideology in education* (pp. 487–511). Oxford: Oxford University Press.

Bourdieu, P. (1991). *Language and symbolic power* (J. B. Thompson, Ed., G. Raymond & M. Adamson, Trans.). Cambridge, MA: Harvard University Press.

Bourdieu, P., & Passeron, J. (1990). *Reproduction in education, society, and culture*. Thousand Oaks, CA: Sage. First published in 1977.

Bové, P. (2005). Continuing the conversation. In H. Bhabha & W. J. T. Mitchell (Eds.), *Edward Said: Continuing the conversation* (pp. 36–42). Chicago: The University of Chicago Press.

Bowles, S., & Gintis, H. (1976). *Schooling in capitalist America*. New York: Basic Books.

Brennan, T. (2005). Resolution. In H. Bhabha & W. J. T. Mitchell (Eds.), *Edward Said: Continuing the conversation* (pp. 43–55). Chicago: The University of Chicago Press.

Brown, A. (2011). "Same old stories": The Black male in social science and educational literature, 1930s to the present. *Teachers College Record*, *113*(9), 2047–2079.

Buras, K. (2008). *Rightist multiculturalism*. New York: Routledge.

Burman, E. (2017). Fanon's other children: Psychopolitical and pedagogical implications. *Race Ethnicity and Education*, *20*(1), 42–56.

Césaire, A. (2000). *Discourse on colonialism*. New York: Monthly Review Press. First published in 1955.

Cmiel, K. (1994). "A broad fluid language of democracy": Discovering the American idiom. In D. Thelen & F. E. Hoxie (Eds.), *Discovering America: Essays on the search for an identity* (pp. 79–102). Urbana: University of Illinois Press.

Collins, P. H. (2000). *Black feminist thought: Knowledge, consciousness, and the politics of empowerment* (2nd ed.). New York: Routledge. First published in 1991.

Counts, G. (1932). *Dare the school build a new social order?* New York: The John Day Co.

Crenshaw, K. (1991). Mapping the margins: Intersectionality, identity politics, and the violence against women of color. *Stanford Law Review*, *43*(6), 1241–1299.

Deleuze, G., & Guattari, F. (1983). *Anti-Oedipus: Capitalism and schizophrenia* (R. Hurley, M. Seem, & H. Lane, Trans.). Minneapolis: University of Minnesota Press.

Dewey, J. (1916). *Democracy and education*. New York: The Free Press.

Dewey, J. (1938). *Experience and education*. New York: Palgrave Macmillan.

Dewey, J. (2001). *The school and society & the child and the curriculum*. Mineola, NY: Dover Publications.

Dimitriadis, G. (2006). On the production of expert knowledge: Revisiting Edward Said's work on the intellectual. *Discourse: Studies in the Cultural Politics of Education*, 27(3), 369–382. doi:10.1080/01596300600838835

Dog, M., & Erdoes, R. (1999). Civilize them with a stick. In S. Ferguson (Ed.), *Mapping the social landscape* (pp. 554–562). Mountain View, CA: Mayfield Publishing Company.

Du Bois, W. E. B. (1989). *The souls of Black folk*. New York: Penguin Books. First published in 1904.

Eagleton, T. (1991). *Ideology*. London: Verso.

Eisner, E. (1976). Educational connoisseurship and criticism: Their form and functions in educational evaluation. *Journal of Aesthetic Education*, 10(3–4), 135–150.

Ellison, R. (1952). *Invisible man*. New York: Random House.

Espiritu, A. (2005). *Five faces of exile: The nation and Filipino American intellectuals*. Stanford: Stanford University Press.

Fanon, F. (2005). *The wretched of the earth* (R. Philcox, Trans.). New York: Grove Press. Originally published in 1961.

Fanon, F. (2008). *Black skin, White masks* (R. Philcox, Trans.). New York: Grove Press. Originally published in 1952.

Ferguson, A. (2001). *Bad boys*. Ann Arbor: University of Michigan Press.

Flecha, R. (1999). Modern and postmodern racism in Europe: Dialogical approach and anti-racist pedagogies. *Harvard Educational Review*, 69(2), 150–171.

Foucault, M. (1977). *Discipline and punish* (A. Sheridan, Trans.). New York: Vintage Books.

Foucault, M. (1980). *Power/knowledge* (C. Gordon, Ed.). New York: Pantheon Books.

Foucault, M. (1991). What is an author? In C. Mukerji & M. Schudson (Eds.), *Rethinking popular culture* (pp. 446–464). Berkeley: University of California Press.

Fraser, N. (1997). *Justice interruptus*. New York: Routledge.

Freire, P. (1993). *Pedagogy of the oppressed* (M. Ramos, Trans.). New York: Continuum. First published in 1970.

Freire, P. (1994). *Pedagogy of hope* (R. Barr, Trans.). New York: Continuum.
Freire, P. (1998). *Paulo Freire reader* (A. M. A. Freire & D. Macedo, Eds.). New York: Continuum.
Freire, P., & Faundez, A. (1989). *Learning to question: A pedagogy of liberation*. New York: Continuum.
Freire, P., & Macedo, D. (1987). *Literacy: Reading the word and the world*. South Hadley, MA: Bergin & Garvey.
Giroux, H. (1983). *Theory and resistance: A pedagogy for the opposition*. Westport, CT: Bergin & Garvey.
Giroux, H. (1988). *Teachers as intellectuals*. Westport, CT: Bergin & Garvey.
Giroux, H. (1992). *Border crossings*. New York: Routledge.
Giroux, H. (1999). Rethinking cultural politics and radical pedagogy in the work of Antonio Gramsci. *Educational Theory*, 49(1), 1–19.
Giroux, H., & McLaren, P. (1986). Teacher education and the politics of engagement: The case for democratic schooling. *Harvard Educational Review*, 56(3), 10–35.
Gottesman, I. (2016). *The critical turn in education: From Marxist critique to poststructuralist feminism to critical theories of race*. New York: Routledge.
Gramsci, A. (1971). *Selections from the prison notebooks* (Q. Hoare & G. Smith Eds. and Trans.). New York: International Publishers.
Grosfoguel, R. (2007). The epistemic decolonial turn: Beyond political-economy paradigms. *Cultural Studies*, 21(2), 211–223.
Hall, S. (1996). The problem of ideology: Marxism without guarantees. In D. Morley & K. Chen (Eds.), *Stuart Hall* (pp. 25–46). London: Routledge.
Harding, S. (1991). *Whose science? Whose knowledge?* Ithaca, NY: Cornell University Press.
Harris, A., & Leonardo, Z. (2018). Intersectionality, race-gender subordination, and education. *Review of Research in Education*, 42, 1–27.
Harris, W. T. (1898). *Psychologic foundations of education*. New York: D. Appleton Publishers.
Hartsock, N. (1987, Fall). Rethinking modernism: Minority vs. majority theories. *Cultural Critique*, 7, 187–206.
He, M. F. (2010). Exile pedagogy: Teaching in-between. In J. Sandlin, B. Schultz, & J. Burdick (Eds.), *Handbook of public pedagogy* (pp. 469–482). New York: Routledge.
Hirsch, E. D. Jr. (1999). *The schools we need: And why we don't have them*. New York: Anchor Books.
hooks, b. (1994). *Teaching to transgress*. New York: Routledge.
Horkheimer, M. (1972). *Critical theory: Selected essays* (M. O'Connell and others, Trans.). New York: Continuum.

REFERENCES

Horkheimer, M., & Adorno, T. (1976). *Dialectic of enlightenment* (J. Cumming, Trans.). New York: Continuum.

Howard, G. (2006). *We can't teach what we don't know: White teachers, multiracial schools* (2nd ed.). New York: Teachers College Press.

Ignatiev, N., & Garvey, J. (1996). Abolish the White race: By any means necessary. In N. Ignatiev & J. Garvey (Eds.), *Race traitor* (pp. 9–14). New York: Routledge.

Jameson, F. (1988). *The ideologies of theory* (Vol. 2). Minneapolis: University of Minnesota Press.

Kelley, R. (1998). *Yo' Mama's disfunktional! Fighting the culture wars in urban America.* Boston: Beacon Press.

Kliebard, H. (2004). *The struggle for the American curriculum 1893–1958* (3rd ed.). New York: Routledge and Kegan Paul.

Kuhn, T. (1970). *The structure of scientific revolutions.* Chicago: The University of Chicago Press.

Laclau, E., & Mouffe, C. (2001). *Hegemony and socialist strategy.* London: Verso.

Ladson-Billings, G., & Tate IV, W. F. (1995). Toward a critical race theory of education. *Teachers College Record, 97*(1), 47–68.

Lather, P. (1991). *Getting smart: Feminist research and pedagogy with/in the postmodern.* New York: Routledge.

Lave, J., & Wenger, E. (1991). *Situated learning.* Cambridge: Cambridge University Press.

Leonardo, Z. (2003a). Interpretation and the problem of domination: Paul Ricoeur's hermeneutics. *Studies in Philosophy and Education, 22*(5), 329–350.

Leonardo, Z. (2003b). Reality on trial: Notes on ideology, education, and Utopia. *Policy Futures in Education, 1*(3), 504–525.

Leonardo, Z. (2003c). Resisting capital: Simulationist and socialist strategies. *Critical Sociology, 29*(2), 211–236.

Leonardo, Z. (2004). Critical social theory and transformative knowledge: The functions of criticism in quality education. *Educational Researcher, 33*(6), 11–18.

Leonardo, Z. (2005). Through the multicultural glass: Althusser, ideology, and race relations in post-civil rights America. *Policy Futures in Education, 3*(4), 400–412.

Leonardo, Z. (2006). *Coloring Paulo Freire: Race and critical pedagogy in the American context.* AERA Annual Conference, San Francisco, CA.

Leonardo, Z. (2007). The war on schools: NCLB, nation creation, and the educational construction of whiteness. *Race Ethnicity & Education, 10*(3), 261–278.

Leonardo, Z. (2010). Whiteness and New Orleans: Racio-economic analysis and the politics of urban space. In Afterword to K. Buras, J. Randels, K. ya Salaam, & Students at the Center (Eds.), *Pedagogy, policy, and the privatized city: Stories of dispossession and defiance from New Orleans* (pp. 159–162). New York: Teachers College Press.

Leonardo, Z. (2012). The 2011 R. Freeman Butts lecture. The race for class: Reflections on a critical raceclass theory of education. *Educational Studies*, 48(5), 427–449.

Leonardo, Z. (2013). *Race frameworks: A multidimensional theory of racism and education.* New York: Teachers College Press.

Leonardo, Z. (2015). Contracting race: Writing, racism, and education. *Critical Studies in Education*, 56(1), 86–98.

Leonardo, Z. (2016a). Tropics of whiteness: Metaphor and the literary turn in White studies. *Whiteness and Education*, 1(1), 3–14.

Leonardo, Z. (2016b). Educational criticism as a new specialization. *Research in Education*, 1(1), 1–6. doi:10.1177/0034523716664604

Leonardo, Z., & Boas, E. (2013). Other kids' teachers: What children of color learn from White women and what this says about race, whiteness, and gender. In M. Lynn & A. Dixson (Eds.), *Handbook of critical race theory and education* (pp. 313–324). New York: Routledge.

Leonardo, Z., & Broderick, A. (2011). Smartness as property: A critical exploration of intersections between whiteness and disability studies. *Teachers College Record*, 113(10), 2206–2232.

Leonardo, Z., & Grubb, W. N. (2019). *Education and racism: A primer on issues and dilemmas* (2nd ed.). New York: Routledge.

Leonardo, Z., & Hunter, M. (2007). Imagining the urban: The politics of race, class, and schooling. In W. Pink & G. Noblit (Eds.), *International handbook of urban education* (pp. 779–802). Dordrecht, The Netherlands: Springer.

Leonardo, Z., & Porter, R. K. (2010). Pedagogy of fear: Toward a Fanonian theory of "safety" in race dialogue. *Race Ethnicity & Education*, 13(2), 139–157.

Leonardo, Z., & Singh, M. (2017). Fanon, education, and the fact of coloniality. In T. Gale & K. Gulson (Eds.), *Education policy and social inequality* (pp. 91–110). London: Springer.

Leonardo, Z., & Vafai, M. (2016). Citizenship education and the colonial contract: The elusive search for social justice in U.S. education. In A. Peterson, R. Hattam, M. Zembylas, & J. Arthur (Eds.), *The Palgrave international handbook of education for citizenship and social justice* (pp. 613–634). New York: Palgrave Macmillan.

Lipsitz, G. (1998). *The possessive investment in whiteness*. Philadelphia: Temple University Press.

Lukács, G. (1971). *History and class consciousness* (R. Livingstone, Trans.). Cambridge, MA: The MIT Press.

Lyotard, J. (1992). *The differend* (G. Abbeele, Trans.). Minneapolis: University of Minnesota Press.

Macavoy, A. (2019). Amid protests, astronomers lose observation time. *ABC News*. Retrieved from https://abcnews.go.com/Technology/wireStory/amid-protest-hawaii-astronomers-lose-observation-time-64901093

Maldonado-Torres, N. (2007). On the coloniality of being: Contributions to the development of a concept. *Cultural Studies*, *21*(20–23), 240–270.

McConaghy, C. (2006). Schooling out of place. *Discourse: Studies in the Cultural Politics of Education*, *27*(3), 325–339. doi:10.1080/01596300600838777

McGrew, K. (2011). A review of class-based theories of student resistance in education: Mapping the origins and influence of *Learning to Labor* by Paul Willis. *Review of Educational Research*, *81*(2), 234–266.

McLaren, P. (1995). *Critical pedagogy and predatory culture: Oppositional politics in a postmodern era*. New York: Routledge.

McLaren, P. (2015). *Life in schools*. New York: Routledge.

McLaren, P., & Scatamburlo-D'Annibale, V. (2005). Class dismissed: Historical materialism and the politics of difference. In Z. Leonardo (Ed.), *Critical pedagogy and race* (pp. 1241–1257). Malden, MA: Blackwell.

Merleau-Ponty, M. (1963). *The structure of behavior*. Pittsburgh, PA: Duquesne University Press.

Mignolo, W. (2002). The geopolitics of knowledge and the colonial difference. *The South Atlantic Quarterly*, *101*(1), 57–96.

Mills, C. (1997). *The racial contract*. Ithaca: Cornell University Press.

Mills, C. (1998). *Blackness visible: Essays on philosophy and race*. Ithaca: Cornell University Press.

Mills, C. (2003). *From class to race: Essays in White Marxism and Black radicalism*. Lanham, MD: Rowman & Littlefield.

Mills, C. (2007). White ignorance. In S. Sullivan & N. Tuana (Eds.), *Race and epistemologies of ignorance* (pp. 13–38). Albany: State University of New York Press.

Mitchell, W. J. T. (2005). Secular divination: Edward Said's humanism. In H. Bhabha & W. J. T. Mitchell (Eds.), *Edward Said: Continuing the conversation* (pp. 99–108). Chicago: The University of Chicago Press.

Mufti, A. (2005). Global comparativism. In H. Bhabha & W. J. T. Mitchell (Eds.), *Edward Said: Continuing the conversation* (pp. 109–126). Chicago: The University of Chicago Press.

Murray, D. W. (1993). What is the western concept of the self: On forgetting David Hume. *Ethos*, *21*(1), 3–23.

Nieto, S. (2003). *Affirming diversity* (4th ed.). New York: Longman.

Nixon, J. (2006). Towards a Hermeneutics of Hope: The legacy of Edward W. Said. *Discourse: Studies in the Cultural Politics of Education*, *27*(3), 341–356. doi:10.1080/01596300600838793

Oliver, M., & Shapiro, T. (1997). *Black wealth, White wealth: A new perspective on racial inequality*. New York: Routledge.

Paperson, L. (2010). The postcolonial Ghetto: Seeing her shape and his hand. *Berkeley Review of Education*, *1*(1), 5–34. Retrieved July 22, 2019, from http://escholarship.org/uc/ucbgse_bre

Pateman, C. (1988). *The sexual contract*. Stanford: Stanford University Press.

Pateman, C., & Mills, C. (2007). *Contract and domination*. New York: Polity Press.

Picheta, R. (2019, April 2). *The first Black hole to be photographed now has a name*. Retrieved from www.cnn.com/2019/04/12/world/black-hole-name-powehi-scli-intl/index.html

Pinar, W. (1981). The reconceptualization of curriculum studies. In H. Giroux, A. Penna, & W. Pinar (Eds.), *Curriculum & instruction* (pp. 87–97). Berkeley: McCutchan Publishing Corporation.

Portes, A., & Rumbaut, R. (2001). *Legacies*. Berkeley: University Press of California Press.

Prior, R. (2019). Hundreds of native Hawaiians gather to protest the construction of a telescope on a sacred mountain. *CNN News*. Retrieved from www.cnn.com/2019/07/15/us/thirty-mile-telescope-mauna-kea-protest-trnd/index.html

Quijano, A. (2000). Coloniality of power, Eurocentrism, and Latin America. *Nepantla*, *1*(3), 533–580.

Ricoeur, P. (1981). *Hermeneutics and the human sciences* (J. B. Thompson, Ed.). Cambridge: Cambridge University Press.

Ricoeur, P. (2007). *The conflict of interpretations*. Chicago: Northwestern University Press.

Rizvi, F., & Lingard, B. (2006). Edward Said and the cultural politics of education. *Discourse: Studies in the Cultural Politics of Education*, *27*(3), 293–308. doi:10.1080/01596300600838744

Roediger, D. (1991). *The wages of whiteness*. New York: Verso.

Roediger, D. (1994). *Toward the abolition of whiteness*. New York: Verso.

Roman, L. G. (2006). This earthly world: Edward Said, the praxis of secular humanisms and situated cosmopolitanisms. *Discourse: Studies in the Cultural Politics of Education*, *27*(3), 357–368. doi:10.1080/01596300600838827

Rousseau, J. (1979). *Emile: Or on education* (A. Bloom, Trans.). New York: Basic Books.

Said, E. (1978). *Orientalism*. New York: Random House.

Said, E. (1983). *The world, the text, and the critic*. Cambridge, MA: Harvard University Press.

Said, E. (1985). *Beginnings: Intention and method*. London: Granta.

Said, E. (1994a). *Culture and imperialism*. New York: Vintage Books.

Said, E. (1994b). *Representations of the intellectual*. New York: Vintage Books.

Said, E. (1999). *Out of place: A memoir*. London: Granta Books.

Said, E. (2000). *Reflections on exile*. Cambridge, MA: Harvard University Press.

Said, E. (2001). *Power, politics, and culture: Interviews with Edward Said*. New York: Vintage Books.

Said, E. (2004). *Humanism and democratic criticism*. New York: Palgrave Macmillan.

Schlesinger, J. (1998). *The disuniting of America: Reflections on a multicultural society* (2nd ed.). New York: W.W. & Norton.

Sider, K. (2019). *White double-consciousness: A critical analysis of discourse in teacher education*. Lanham, MD: Lexington Books.

Singh, M., & Greenlaw, J. (1998). Postcolonial theory in the literature classroom: Contrapuntal readings. Literary theory in the high school English classroom. *Theory into Practice*, *37*(3), 193–202.

Sleeter, C. (1993). How White teachers construct race. In C. McCarthy & W. Crichlow (Eds.), *Race, identity, and representation in education* (pp. 157–171). New York: Routledge.

Smith, D. (1989). *The everyday world as problematic*. Boston: Northeastern University Press.

Smith, L. T. (1999). *Decolonizing methodologies*. London: Zed Books.

Spring, J. (2000). *Deculturalization and the struggle for equality* (3rd ed.). Boston: McGraw-Hill.

Swartz, E. (1992). Emancipatory narratives: Rewriting the master script in the school curriculum. *Journal of Negro Education*, *61*(3), 341–355.

Symcox, L. (2002). *Whose history? The struggle for national standards in American classrooms*. New York: Teachers College Press.

Symes, C. (2006). The paradox of the canon: Edward W. Said and musical transgression. *Discourse: Studies in the Cultural Politics of Education*, *27*(3), 309–324. doi:10.1080/01596300600838751

Thompson, J. (1984). *Studies in the theory of ideology*. Berkeley: University of California Press.

Tuck, E., & Yang, K. (2012). Decolonization is not a metaphor. *Decolonization: Indigeneity, Education & Society*, *1*(1), 1–40.

Uhrmacher, P. B., Moroye, C., & Flinders, C. (2017). *Using educational criticism and connoisseurship for qualitative research*. New York: Routledge.

Valenzuela, A. (1999). *Subtractive schooling: US-Mexican youth and the politics of caring*. Albany: State University of New York Press.

Van Dyke, M. (2019). Hawaiian protesters started a school on Mauna Kea to teach local culture to the next generation. *NBC News*. Retrieved from www.nbcnews.com/news/us-news/hawaiian-protesters-started-school-mauna-kea-teach-local-culture-next-n1038911

Vico, (1984). *The new science*. T. G. Bergin and M. H. Fisch (Trans.). Ithaca, NY: Cornell University Press.

Villenas, S. (2010). Thinking Latina(o) education with and from Chicana/Latina feminist cultural studies: Emerging pathways – decolonial possibilities. In Z. Leonardo (Ed.), *Handbook of cultural politics and education* (pp. 451–476). Dordrecht, The Netherlands: Sense Publishers.

Volosinov, V. (2006). *Marxism and the philosophy of language*. Cambridge, MA: Harvard University Press.

Vygotsky, L. (1978). *Mind in society*. 4th ed. Cambridge, MA: Harvard University Press.

Washington, B. T. (1986). *Up from slavery*. New York: Penguin Books.

Weiler. K. (1994). *Women teaching for change*. Westport, CT: Bergin & Garvey.

Williams, R. (1977). *Marxism and literature*. Oxford: Oxford University Press.

Willis, P. (1977). *Learning to labor*. New York: Columbia University Press.

Willis, P. (1981). Cultural production is different from cultural reproduction is different from social reproduction is different from reproduction. *Interchange*, *12*(2–3), 48–67.

Yancy, G. (2012). *Look, a White!* Philadelphia: Temple University Press.

INDEX

30-meter telescope (TMT) 34

Adele 55
administrative colonialism 14
affiliation 110
ageism 74
Alger, Horatio 58
Alt-Right 15–16
American Educational Research Association (AERA) 2–3
American Orientalism 50–51
anti-intellectuals 47–54; teachers as 28–54
Anti-Oedipus (Deleuze and Guattari) 65
Anyon, Jean 88–89
Apple, Michael 88
Aquino, Corazon 55
Arabization 21
Area Studies 49
Arnold, Matthew 22, 49, 66, 106
Austen, Jane 63

Ball, Stephen 88
Banks, James 11–12, 99
Baudrillard, Jean 95
beginnings 107–110, 115
Beginnings: Intention and Method (Said) 107–108
Bellow, Saul 22, 105

Benjamin, Walter 90, 100
Black boys and men 71
black holes 34–35, 37
Blacks 71, 73, 81, 96
Bloom, Allan 11–12, 105
Bloom, Benjamin 90
Bobbitt, John F. 3, 9
border pedagogy 26
Brown, Anthony 96
Butler, Judith 101

chauvinism, reverse 65
Chomsky, Noam 5, 23–24
Citibank 99
CoIntelPro 44
Coloma, Roland 89
colonial difference 23
Colonial-Imperial Project 12–17
colonialism 14–15, 18–19, 37, 52–53, 58; administrative 14; in literature and language 63–64; official 39–40; posting up on 38–47
coloniality 12–14; dis-orienting 1–27; of power 14
Columbia University 4
contrapuntal analysis 19–20, 84–119
contrapuntal education and criticism 91–114, 116–117
contrapuntality 93–94, 116–117

Counts, George 3
critical educational policy analysis 88
Critical Pedagogy 2, 86–90
critical raceclass theory 2
Critical Race Theory 2, 87–88
critical theory 89–90
Critical University Studies 16
criticism 86–87; as an act of freedom 114–119; contrapuntal 91–114, 116–117; educational 5–6, 84–119; literary 86, 93; Said's project 91–98, 102–103; *see also Humanism and Democratic Criticism* (Said); *World, the Text, and the Critic, The* (Said)
CRT *see* Critical Race Theory
cult of ethnicity 11–12
cultural wars 11–12, 51–52
culture: home 70; popular 22; Said on *see Culture and Imperialism* (Said); *Power, Politics, and Culture: Interviews with Edward Said* (Said)
"Culture" 49, 66, 106
Culture and Imperialism (Said) 41–42, 52–53, 64, 67
curriculum: dis-orienting 1–27; traveling 22–27
Curriculum, The (Bobbitt) 9
curriculum studies 3, 9–12

Decolonial Group 22–23
Decolonization Movement 22–27
Decolonizing Methodologies (Smith) 110–111
democratic criticism *see Humanism and Democratic Criticism* (Said)
demographics 77
Desert Storm 46, 50–51
Dewey, John 3, 9
Discipline and Punish (Foucault) 12–13, 50
discovery, scientific 35–36

Eagleton, Terry 2
"East is East" 75–76

education: contrapuntal 91–114; *herrenvolk* system 100
educational criticism 5–6, 84–119; building 87–91; contrapuntal 91–114
educational psychology 86
Egypt 12
Eisner, Elliot 84–85, 89–90
elitism 22
English Orientalism 50–51
Enlightenment 100
Eno, Brian 28
epistemic problem 17–22
epistemology, Western 18–19
era of the exile 58–59
Espiritu, August 56
ethnicity, cult of 11–12
Eurocentrism 18–20, 23
Euro-humanism 101
exile 55–56; development of 67–76; era of 58–59; forms of 58; hermeneutics of 57; pedagogies of 2–3, 55–83; personality of 62–66; refuge in 57–62; Said on *see Reflections on Exile* (Said)
existentialism 110
expert(ise): problem of 31–37, 46; reconstruction of 28–54; teacher 32–33

false consciousness 103–104
Far Right 15
Faundez, Antonio 77–78
feminist theory 88
Ferguson, Ann 71
filiation 109–110
Fitzgerald, F. Scott 67
France 99–100; French Orientalism 51
Frankfurt School 22, 31, 55, 90–91
Fraser, Nancy 12
Frazier, E. Franklin 96
freedom 114–119
Freire, Paulo 2–3, 56, 75–80, 82; *Pedagogy of the Oppressed* 2, 86–87
French Orientalism 51

Gillborn, Dave 88
Giroux, Henry 14, 29, 87, 100
Goldberg, David T. 101
Gramsci, Antonio 7–8, 29
Great Britain 99–100; English Orientalism 50–51
Gulson, Kal 88

Hall, Stuart 108–109, 114
Harris, William Torrey 10–11
Harvard University 4
Heart of Darkness (Conrad) 63
Hemingway, Ernest 67
herrenvolk educational system 100
Hirsch, E. D., Jr. 7–8
Hollywood 46
home 67–76
home culture 70
Howard, Gary 78
Hugo of St. Victor 61
humanism 8–9, 74, 89, 99–101, 111–112, 118–119; Euro-humanism 101; military 99
Humanism and Democratic Criticism (Said) 64, 92–95, 98–100, 111–112, 118

identity politics 113
ideological state apparatus (ISA) 17
imperialism 6–7, 12, 22; in literature and language 63–64; Said on *see Culture and Imperialism* (Said)
indigenous or native people 12–13, 61
intellectuals 29; amateur 24, 29, 38–39, 43, 48–49; policy 38–39; representative 47; role and function of 31, 47–49; Said on *see Representations of the Intellectual* (Said); teachers as anti-intellectuals 28–54; theories of 47–48
intersectionality 115
Israel-Palestine conflict 19–20, 57, 94

Jameson, Fredric 9
Johnson, Dwayne "The Rock" 34
Journal of Aesthetic Education 84–85

Keck telescope 35–36
Kelley, Robin D. G. 51–52
Kim (Kipling) 63
Kliebard, Herbert M. 11
knowledge 17–22; official 11–12; religious 107; sacred 106; traveler's 20; Western 1–27
Kuhn, Thomas 114

labeling or naming 36–37
language 95–96, 98
Lather, Patti 100
learning: in and out of place 55–83; to question 82
Left 47–49
Lewis, Bernard 46, 49
Lingard, Bob 88
Lipman, Pauline 88
literary criticism 86, 93
literature and language 63–64

Maldonado-Torres, Nelson 14
Marcos, Fernando 55
Marxism 2, 13, 20, 23, 88–89, 97, 103–104, 108–109
Mauna Kea Mountain (Hawaii) 33–34
McLaren, Peter 14, 88–89
Middle East 46, 50–51
Mignolo, Walter 23
military humanism 99
Mills, Charles 2, 19, 42–43, 100–101
Mimesis (Aeurbach) 5, 64
Montclair State University, New Jersey 87
Moynihan Report 51, 96
multiculturalism 19, 99
Murray, D. W. 8–9

naming or labeling 36–37
Napoleon 12
nationalism 19, 21, 62, 66

INDEX

Native Americans 27, 57
natives 12–13, 61
NATO 99
New Right 16
New Science, The (Vico) 5, 17, 64
Nostromo (Conrad) 63

Obama, Barack 43
Occidentalism 21, 65, 113–114
official knowledge 11–12
Orientalism 22, 29, 50–51, 95–96, 113–114; history of 4–5; inversion of 21; urban 51–52
Orientalism (Said) 1–7, 38, 41–47, 50, 101
Orientalism Now 45–46
Oumuamuas 36
Out of Place (Said) 67

Pakistanis 75–76
Palestine 19–20, 57, 76, 94
pedagogy: border 26; Critical Pedagogy 2, 86–90; of exile 2–3, 55–83
Pedagogy of the Oppressed (Freire) 2, 86–87
policy intellectuals 38–39
politics: identity 113; of naming or labeling 36–37; Said on *see Power, Politics, and Culture: Interviews with Edward Said* (Said)
popular culture 22
populism 117–118
postcolonial analysis 4–5, 13–14, 39–42
post-humanism 112
post-intellectuals 47–54
postmodernism 21–22
Powehi 34, 37
Power, Politics, and Culture: Interviews with Edward Said (Said) 31–33, 38–40, 48–49, 53–54, 67–68
Princeton University 4
professionalism 33
provincialism, intellectual 22

psychology, educational 86
Puuhonua o Puuhuluhulu University 36

questioning 82
Quijano, Anibal 14

racio-economic analysis 2
racism 5, 71–72; intrinsic vs. extrinsic 65–66; reverse 65
Ranciere, J. 100
recycled discourse 96
Reflections on Exile (Said) 24–26, 29, 38–40, 52, 55–56, 59–72, 81, 93–94
refugees 67–68
religiosity 105–106
religious knowledge 107
Representations of the Intellectual (Said) 29–32, 38, 48, 57, 87
representative intellectuals 47
reverse chauvinism 65
reverse racism 65
Ricoeur, Paul 2
Rizvi, Fazal 88
Roediger, David 2
ruralism 57

sacred knowledge 106
sacred texts 50
Safire, William 32
Said, Edward Wadie 56; biography 3–4, 24–25; Palestinian identity 61; self-characterization 113; *see also specific works by title*
Sanders, Bernie 34
scientific discovery 35–36
self-abnegation 10
Shavit, Ari 67–68
Sleeter, Christine 78
smartness 42–43
Smith, Linda Tuhiwai 89, 110–111
Socrates 79
Solorzano, Danny 89
Spielberg, Stephen 46

teachers: as anti-intellectuals 28–54; education of 86; as experts 32–33; public perception of 32–33; White 76–83
Teachers College Record 88
theory, traditional vs. critical 90
TMT (30-meter telescope) 34–36
touching mode 94
traditional theory 90
travelers 20, 69–70
traveling curriculum 22–27
traveling theory 40–41
Trump, Donald 42–43, 119

United States 99–100; American Orientalism 50–51; cultural wars 51–52; Desert Storm 46, 50–51
University of Hawaii 36
University of St. Thomas, Minnesota 87
urban Orientalism 51–52

van den Berghe, Pierre 100

Washington, Booker T. 89
Western epistemology 18–19
Western knowledge 1–27
White habitus 80–81
White teachers 76–83
Whitman, Walt 117
Williams, Raymond 61, 108–109
Williams, William Appleman 14, 72
Willis, Paul 104, 108–109
worldliness 99–100
World, the Text, and the Critic, The (Said) 40–41, 65, 69–70, 97, 101–106, 110, 113, 116

Yang, Wayne 70
Yiannopoulos, Milo 15–16
Yugoslavia 99